Paul A. Sommers, PhD

Consumer Satisfaction in Medical Practice

Pre-publication
REVIEWS,
COMMENTARIES,
EVALUATIONS . . .

"**C**onsumer approaches to delivering care will dominate the future of health care. Paul Sommers shows the gulf existing between the conventional wisdom on medical practice and consumer interests. He then shows ways for the foresighted to make medical practices exemplary examples of consumer-driven organizations. His unique approach is perceptive, businesslike, and scientifically sound."

Richard Hamer
Director,
Interstudy Publications,
Minneapolis, MN

"**T**he key to the usefulness of this book is contained in its title. 'Consumers' are the focus, and Dr. Sommers views the medical practice from a marketing and public relations perspective. The health care environment is becoming more and more competitive, with patients shopping around for the best coverage at the lowest cost. To distinguish a practice in the marketplace one must define value, and what constitutes value in a medical practice. Today, value has to mean more than medical treatment. It has to extend to all aspects of delivering that treatment, and the future success of any medical practice will depend on the satisfaction of its customers. Dr. Sommers offers effective ways to reorient a practice to deliver quality care and measure the satisfaction of patients.

The Haworth Press, Inc.

Consumer Satisfaction in Medical Practice

HAWORTH Marketing Resources
Innovations in Practice & Professional Services
William J. Winston, Senior Editor

New, Recent, and Forthcoming Titles:

Managing Sales Professionals: The Reality of Profitability by Joseph P. Vaccaro

Squeezing a New Service into a Crowded Market by Dennis J. Cahill

Publicity for Mental Health Clinicians: Using TV, Radio, and Print Media to Enhance Your Public Image by Douglas H. Ruben

Managing a Public Relations Firm for Growth and Profit by A. C. Croft

Utilizing the Strategic Marketing Organization: The Modernization of the Marketing Mindset by Joseph P. Stanco

Internal Marketing: Your Company's Next Stage of Growth by Dennis J. Cahill

The Clinician's Guide to Managed Behavioral Care by Norman Winegar

Marketing Health Care into the Twenty-First Century: The Changing Dynamic by Alan K. Vitberg

Fundamentals of Strategic Planning for Health-Care Organizations edited by Stan Williamson, Robert Stevens, David Loudon, and R. Henry Migliore

Risky Business: Managing Violence in the Workplace by Lynne Falkin McClure

Predicting Successful Hospital Mergers and Acquisitions: A Financial and Marketing Analytical Tool by David P. Angrisani and Robert L. Goldman

Marketing Research That Pays Off: Case Histories of Marketing Research Leading to Success in the Marketplace edited by Larry Percy

How Consumers Pick a Hotel: Strategic Segmentation and Target Marketing by Dennis Cahill

Applying Telecommunications and Technology from a Global Business Perspective by Jay Zajas and Olive Church

Strategic Planning for Private Higher Education by Carle M. Hunt, Kenneth W. Oosting, Robert Stevens, David Loudon, and R. Henry Migliore

Writing for Money in Mental Health by Douglas H. Ruben

The New Business Values for Success in the Twenty-First Century: Improvement, Innovation, Inclusion, Incentives, Information by John Persico and Patricia Rouner Morris

Marketing Planning Guide, Second Edition by Robert E. Stevens, David L. Loudon, Bruce Wrenn, and William E. Warren

Contemporary Sales Force Management by Tony Carter

4 × 4 Leadership and the Purpose of the Firm by H. H. Pete Bradshaw

Lessons in Leisure Business Success: The Recreation Professional's Business Transformation Primer by Jonathan T. Scott

Guidebook to Managed Care and Practice Management Terminology by Norman Winegar and Michelle L. Hayter

Medical Group Management in Turbulent Times: How Physician Leadership Can Optimize Health Plan, Hospital, and Medical Group Performance by Paul A. Sommers

Defining Your Market: Winning Strategies for High-Tech, Industrial, and Service Firms by Art Weinstein

Alignment: A Provider's Guide to Managing the Practice of Health Care by Paul A. Sommers

Consumer Satisfaction in Medical Practice by Paul A. Sommers

Using Public Relations Strategies to Promote Your Nonprofit Organization by Ruth Ellen Kinzey

The Aftermath of Reengineering: Downsizing and Corporate Performance by Tony Carter

Principles of Advertising: A Global Perspective by Monle Lee and Carla Johnson

Consumer Satisfaction in Medical Practice

Paul A. Sommers, PhD

The Haworth Press
New York • London • Oxford

The Haworth Press, Inc., 10 Alice Street, Binghamton, NY 13904-1580

Cover design by Marylouise E. Doyle.

Library of Congress Cataloging-in-Publication Data

Sommers, Paul A.
   Consumer satisfaction in medical practice / Paul A. Sommers.
      p.   cm.
   Includes bibliographical references and index.
   ISBN 0-7890-0713-4 (alk. paper)
   1. Patient satisfaction. 2. Medicine—Practice—Quality control. 3. Medical care—Evaluation. 4. Consumer satisfaction. I. Title. [DNLM: 1. Practice Management, Medical. 2. Consumer Satisfaction. W 80 S697c 1999]
   R727.3.S66   1999
   362.1′068′5—DC21
DNLM/DLC
for Library of Congress   98-54478
                                                                                                          CIP

CONTENTS

ABOUT THE AUTHOR

Paul A. Sommers, PhD, is Vice President of the Data Services Organization for Ingenix/United HealthCare, Inc. in Minneapolis, Minnesota. He is also Adjunct Professor of Health Policy and Management in the Carlson School of Management at the University of Minnesota, Minneapolis, and Preceptor for MBA students in Medical Group Management at the University of St. Thomas Graduate School, also in Minneapolis. Over the past twenty-two years, Dr. Sommers has served with various medical groups and integrated health systems such as the Marshfield Clinic in Marshfield, Wisconsin; the Gundersen Clinic in LaCrosse, Wisconsin; the Ramsey Clinic in St. Paul, Minnesota; and Allina Health System/Medica Health Plans in Minneapolis. In addition, he is the author of more than eighty journal articles, textbook chapters, and publications related to health care, including *Medical Group Management in Turbulent Times: How Physician Leadership Can Optimize Health Plan, Hospital, and Medical Group Performance* (The Haworth Press, Inc., 1998) and *Alignment: A Provider's Guide to Managing the Practice of Health Care* (The Haworth Press, Inc., 1999).

Preface

In the past, medical professionals were able to function as a service industry without having to worry too much about addressing the issue of consumer satisfaction. The primary emphasis in medical care rested on the physician-patient relationship, with the physician generally held in high regard by the patient. Patients usually believed that a relatively equal—and high—standard of care could be received from almost all physicians. Very few patients gave much thought to comparative shopping.

In recent years, however, patients have begun to ask for a greater voice in their own health care. They now see themselves as consumers of health care and, as consumers, have begun to question, along with their payers, both the quality of the care they receive and its cost. The result has been a growing demand for care of good quality at less cost. That, in turn, has led to increased competition among health care providers.

In light of these trends, health care professionals must change their old ways of doing business. Consumer satisfaction will play only a bigger and bigger role in medical practice, as patients and their families, referring physicians, and payer sources become more selective about determining which physicians will be getting their business. This book is intended to equip physicians and other decision makers in health care with the necessary tools to meet the growing demand for consumer satisfaction in medical practice. Using the tools described here must become a way of doing business, if physicians, hospitals, and health plans are going to survive the economic changes projected for the health care professions.

Paul A. Sommers, PhD

Introduction

The practice of medicine has been a confidential and privileged relationship between physician and patient. The nature of the physician-patient interaction is embodied in the Hippocratic Oath, which outlines the duties and obligations of physicians. When a physician enters the business of medical practice, therefore, he or she must run that business in a way that promotes high-quality medical care. That goes without saying.

Yet even high-quality care can be delivered without consumer satisfaction, as indeed it often has been in the past. More and more frequently, however, medical professionals are recognizing the importance of providing high-quality service as well as high-quality care to their patients. They have found that such a consumer-oriented approach makes good business sense. It also goes a long way toward assuring that the patient receives the very best care possible.

Incorporating consumer satisfaction or excellence into a medical practice does not cost the typical physician any more than the old, nonservice-oriented approach. Consumer satisfaction is a style, a total approach, a complete manner in which health care is delivered to achieve excellence. Cost is a non-issue, because it does not cost any more to treat the consumer right the first time he or she comes into the hospital or clinic. In fact, *not* treating the consumer right can be very costly. First, all patients' complaints must be documented and dealt with, which costs time and effort, and second, some of those complaints may develop into expensive malpractice lawsuits. In addition, the dissatisfied consumer may go elsewhere for care, another costly problem. Studies have found that it takes five times as much money to attract a new customer as it does to retain an existing one. By multiplying by five the annual value associated with *one* patient's outpatient and inpatient charges (including lab and X-ray charges) it is easy to see the loss of revenue from one unhappy health care consumer.

Many health care providers are unaware that their patients are dissatisfied with the care they are receiving, because patients seldom complain directly to providers. In fact, research has shown that 96 percent of unhappy customers never complain to the people providing them with a service. But they do tell their families and friends. Research has also shown that each dissatisfied customer tells nine other people about their concerns, and 13 percent tell as many as twenty other people. Word gets around.

Health care is primarily a physician-driven service. Without the voluntary commitment, leadership, and follow-through of physicians in the area of consumer satisfaction, little (if any) progress can be sustained. It is essential, therefore, that physicians take a leading and active role in identifying and implementing the changes that need to occur to make consumer satisfaction a way of doing business in hospitals and medical practices. By caring enough about their patients to make these changes, physicians will find that their patients will remain loyal and will return to them whenever they have a health care problem.

PART I:
UNDERSTANDING CONSUMER
SATISFACTION AS A WAY
OF DOING BUSINESS

Chapter 1

Myths and Other Misunderstandings About Medical Practice

For physicians to thrive instead of just survive in the contemporary marketplace for health care, traditional approaches to medical practice will have to change. Like it or not, physicians are going to have to reexamine—and then discard—the following myths and outdated beliefs about what the practice of medicine is going to be like during the twenty-first century.

Myth #1: Solo Practitioners and Independent Practices Will Dominate the Practice of Medicine

With increasing frequency, independent physicians are going to find it advantageous to consider some form of affiliation with another physician, a group, or a consortium. Such affiliations will benefit independent physicians by helping them obtain malpractice insurance, negotiate with insurance companies and HMOs, share patients within defined specialties, and reduce duplicative overhead costs, including those associated with incorporating consumer satisfaction into the practice.

Myth #2: Medical Practice Will Remain an Entrepreneurial, Small Business

In the past, many medical practices functioned as entrepreneurial, small businesses, but that was before the government, the insurance industry, and other third-party payers declared the 1990s to be "the decade of containing physician costs," much as the 1980s were a watershed for significant cost-containing changes in hospitals. Payers and regulators of health care are fed up with uncontrolled costs and are doing something about it by directing patients to medical practices that are both quality oriented and cost conscious. As a result, reimbursement will decrease for all physicians, which in turn will force practices to de-escalate their costs while keeping quality standards high. To hold down medical and administrative costs while enhancing revenues, physicians will need to think and act more collectively.

Myth #3: "Curing" Patients Is All That Is Needed For Consumers to Feel Satisfied

In the past, physicians had the luxury of practicing medicine without too much concern about how the service was perceived by the patient. In many cases, it was presumed that the patient was just grateful for whatever medicine or related care was received. Indeed, most people perceived service as something they received at a gas station, restaurant, or hotel, but not at a doctor's office.

Times have changed. The medical practices of physicians who have no competition in their specialty in a particular geographic area may survive the changes forecast for the next ten years, but they will probably not thrive—unless those physicians make consumer satisfaction a way of doing business. Of course there will always be exceptions—"one of a kind" medical practices such as those doing organ transplants—but even those physicians will benefit (and so will their patients) if they put consumer-oriented services in place.

As a service industry, the practice of medicine is fast becoming as market-driven as travel, hotels, banking, and a myriad of other industries. Consumers expect high-quality service from all physicians. It is the predominant perception that sways consumers when evaluating physicians. A voluntary commitment to practice excellence in every aspect of care and service to their patients will distinguish the thriving provider from the competition.

Myth #4: Implementing a Consumer Satisfaction Program Takes Too Much Time and Money

Actually, it will be costly *not* to implement such a program, because patients will simply go elsewhere. The specific cost of a con-

sumer satisfaction program depends upon how it is implemented—
the number of personnel involved in surveying patients, for example,
and how surveys will be conducted (by mail, telephone, focus
groups, or a combination of these). Physicians whose practices are
currently without noteworthy competition would be wise to become
consumer oriented now, before the competition arrives. Doing it
now will be less expensive than doing it while dueling with other
physicians for patients.

Myth #5: Once a Physician Has Referred a Patient to Another Physician, He or She Will Continue to Refer Patients to That Physician

A physician who receives a referred patient from another physician should not expect to receive further referrals from that source.
Thus, referring physicians need to be treated as consumers. After
being provided with a high-quality consultation, the referred patient
should be returned to the referring physician in a timely fashion,
along with a clear, concise report aimed at making it easy for the
referring physician to incorporate the information into his or her
planning for that patient's future health care needs. Physicians
should call referring physicians a day or two after sending their
report to see whether they have any questions or concerns.

Myth #6: Consumer Satisfaction Is More Important in Some Medical Settings Than in Others

Too often, less than satisfactory service is rationalized because of
an erroneous belief that in some specific settings, meeting consumers' high expectations for service is not very important. This is not
true. Consumer satisfaction should be the goal of all medical practices, no matter where or under what circumstances the care is
provided—whether inpatient or outpatient, for example, or in a
hospital or a private practice. Physicians need to take the lead
through voluntary commitment to consumer-oriented medical care,
for it offers the greatest potential for attaining consumer satisfaction. Once physicians take the lead in establishing excellence in
care and service, other medical support staff will follow.

Myth #7: A Consumer Satisfaction Program Can Replace Risk Management and Quality Assurance Programs

Wrong. Through its emphasis on making patients and members of their families well-informed and active participants in their medical care, a consumer-oriented service can help minimize the risk of malpractice suits. It does not, however, take the place of a carefully-thought-out program of risk management or quality assurance.

Some medical professionals worry that asking consumers to respond to any kind of questions about their medical care, even ones related only to service, will only cause them to focus on what they did not like about the care, rather than on what they did like. Some even worry that this may lead to more malpractice lawsuits, as consumers begin to think that there must have been something wrong with the care, if the physician is quizzing them about it.

This concern is unmerited. For medical practices to stay competitive, they must find out what their patients do not like, as well as what they like. Only when problems have been clearly identified is it possible to design and implement modifications in service to correct them. The goal is to find out what is wrong, not just what is right. When consumers are convinced that their input is really valued and that the goal of gathering that input is to improve medical services, they will become willing participants.

Myth #8: Attaining Consumer Satisfaction Requires Only Simple "Smile Training" Techniques

Establishing a consumer-oriented approach to medical care requires more than superficial techniques. Physicians and staff alike must be voluntarily committed to establishing excellence and improving their relationship with consumers. They must learn how to become good listeners and how to make sure each patient's needs are met. More often than not, these skills are not recognized as being important, even crucial, in the health care environment.

Yet they are. The St. Paul Fire and Marine Insurance Company has demonstrated that although about one of every hundred hospitalized patients could legally bring an action for negligence against their medical care provider for failing to act or for acting improperly, less than 10 percent of those actually do. Why? The company reported that the answer can be found in the relationships patients have with their health care providers. The more positive and satisfactory the patients perceived those relationships to be, the less likely they were to initiate a lawsuit.

Myth #9: Providing Consumer Satisfaction Is Outdated and Too Expensive

Although it has been talked about for some time, consumer satisfaction has yet to be fully integrated into modern health care practices as a way of doing business. Some physicians believe that they have enough to worry about—especially shrinking reimbursement from Medicare and other payer sources—without spending time and money developing consumer satisfaction programs for their practices.

By putting all their efforts into counteracting government-initiated cost-containment measures, however, physicians are often overlooking the bottom-line benefits of a consumer satisfaction program. Physicians do not have to go overboard to become service oriented. Large expenditures are not needed, either for development of the satisfaction surveys or for the purchase of systems to do the mailing, telephone calls, and collecting and analyzing of data.

What is most needed to become consumer oriented is a voluntary commitment—a commitment to begin thinking about the consumer first. Whether a consumer arrives at a medical facility as a result of a marketing campaign, an ad in the Yellow Pages, or a referral from another professional, the fact remains that the care *and service* he or she receives at the facility will determine whether he or she returns. Furthermore, each satisfied consumer will tell at least five other people, one of whom is quite likely also to choose to use the facility. Establishing excellence in care and service does not represent a line item expense. However, the degree to which excellence exists is perceived by the consumer at each and every encounter with the provider and support staff.

Chapter 2

Looking at Health Care
from the Patient's Perspective

Good health is perhaps one of the most primary desires among humans, along with food, sleep, sex, and the need to feel important. Healthful living has been idolized and sought from time immemorial. Kings, monarchs, and other luminaries have quested for perpetual life as far back in history as records have been kept. A belief in the importance of attaining and maintaining good health is almost universally shared by the world's societies. Thus, it is not surprising that efforts toward public health have been financially supported by government-run social, educational, and health agencies and by hundreds, possibly thousands, of volunteer and lay organizations throughout the world.

Annually, billions of dollars are spent on programs to promote health care and related services. In most cases, the consumer has had little to say in the evaluation of those services. That is now changing. Given the current climate of spiraling medical costs and the intense discussions now underway about a national program of health insurance in the United States, the need to involve those who benefit from health care—consumers—in the evaluation process has become more evident. Yet, although the concept of asking consumers their opinions about the medical care delivery system is not new, it has not been addressed consistently by many health care providers.

So what must be done to ensure that patients are more satisfied with their health care service? To begin with, professionals need to start examining the services they provide, from the patient's viewpoint. Take the office visit as an example. Only 10 percent of the time a patient spends at a doctor's office is directly related to the care sought. Most of the patient's time is spent waiting, filling out forms, or moving from one station to another. The amount of time actually spent with a doctor or nurse—whether for a physical evaluation, undergoing a laboratory test, or being informed about options for treatment—is usually quite limited. Patients have basically resigned themselves to the fact that most trips to the doctor are a waste of time, except for the few minutes they spend with the doctor or nurse.

Because patients have, for the most part, quietly endured long waits at their doctors' offices in the past, some practitioners have come to believe that it is now permissible to let patients sit in their waiting rooms well beyond their scheduled appointment times without even giving them an explanation for the delay. Consumers are becoming increasingly intolerant of such treatment. Indeed, clinicians who fail to give patients and their families appropriate consideration will soon find themselves losing many of their patients to their competitors. Shopping for medical services is now commonplace, and people will not hesitate to travel an extra fifty or seventy-five miles for satisfactory service.

In the fall of 1997, Allina Health System of Minneapolis, Minnesota surveyed the members of its managed care organization, Medica Health Plans, which had more than one million members. Allina wanted to know what its health plan members thought about the doctors, hospitals, quality of care and service, and the amount of choice each patient/health plan member really had. Greenberg Research, Inc. of Washington, DC, conducted a series of focus groups early in 1997 to open up the discussion with Medica members and have the members help design the survey process.[1] One thousand nine hundred sixty-seven members participated in the interviews, taking about twenty-five minutes on the telephone. Results were based on an in-depth study of 1,033 interviews, representative of the whole Allina subscriber population (including oversamples with non-Twin City members) across five insurance products and members with high utilization.

Results illustrated the desire of the health plan members to specifically have a greater voice in the direction the HMO was going and the role its health care resources, the physicians, should be playing. The health plan was not perceived to consult with its members or place a high priority on listening to their views. And, while the physicians are the organization's biggest resource, the members are uncertain of the influence of doctors and their ability to represent patient needs to the health plan.

Significant opportunity was identified because the health care organization was willing to ask its members for input. The voice of the membership and third party payers has long-term consequences, and rightly so—they pay the bills. Value is increased as member inputs become an ongoing part of the process. However, once the inputs have been received, they must be acted on. If ignored, members will vote with their feet—they will leave and join an organization that listens and acts accordingly. In this report, there is strong support for increasing the role of doctors. Broad support is also evident for new processes such as surveys and regular group discussions between members and health plan management. Momentum has created the need for new structures that routinely incorporate member input into patient appeals and coverage decisions. Members are not seeking arbitrary and capricious control, but instead a reliable health care plan that has a strong partnership in place with its physicians and that listens to its users, the members.

EXAMINING THE SYSTEMS FOR DELIVERING SERVICES

Health care delivery is designed around the doctor's schedule. Patients must fit their concerns—their working hours, the hours their children are in school, the distance they must travel from their home or worksite to the doctor's office—into the doctor's schedule. Most medical practices try to assist the patient in finding a convenient time, but doing so is not considered a priority. If an appointment time can be found that does not greatly inconvenience the patient, great. If not, well, perhaps the patient will have better luck next time. In the new competitive climate, however, this type of attitude is not going to be tolerated much longer.

Medical practices could learn a lot about meeting the needs of consumers from studying other businesses that count on consumer satisfaction for their livelihood—motels, hotels, and restaurants, for example. All these businesses are considered service industries, as are health care providers. These services, however, have routinely developed short checklists of questions to ask consumers when they call to make reservations—checklists that help the service provider better meet the needs of the customers. The business thus accommodates the consumer, rather than the other way around. Why can't health care providers do the same?

Hotels, restaurants, and other businesses conduct frequent and thorough surveys to make sure their customers are happy with the service provided, while at the same time identifying accommodations to make their next trip even more enjoyable. Medical practices need to do the same. Although some medical organizations conduct periodic surveys to examine patient satisfaction, relatively few establish and maintain a routine system of such evaluations. The market for health services is highly competitive. To maintain accreditation ratings, hospitals need a certain number of patients to occupy their beds and, to balance their budgets, all medical facilities need a certain number of patients walking through their doors. One would think, therefore, that health care providers would place greater emphasis on the development of a complete consumer-oriented approach to the delivery of care.

ALIGNING SERVICES WITH PATIENTS' NEEDS

By placing oneself in a patient's shoes, it is easier to understand what leads a patient to feel frustrated and dissatisfied with the medical care he or she receives. Too often, for example, patients are expected to follow rigorous directions and procedures. Written orders and paperwork handed to them may be far too complex and detailed. Patients may be given pills for very good reasons, but some fail to understand adequately why they must strictly comply with the recommended dosage. Patients also frequently fail to understand the need for filling out a seemingly endless and often redundant stream of forms and applications.

All current activities and demands made of patients should be examined and, if found to impede favorable service, eliminated if possible, or at least modified. These include not only activities at the nurses' station and at the appointment desk, but also procedures

in the physician's examining room and even paperwork that origi-
nates in the billing or insurance processing offices.

Is Medical Service Being Provided with an Eye on the Consumer's Needs?

Such a question must be asked about all parts of the system. Too
many executive meetings aim discussions at one subject—the need
to see a certain number of patients on a daily, weekly, monthly, or
yearly basis. Yet it is often forgotten that office budgets, profits for
practitioners, and the financial strength of progressive hospitals and
physicians' service organizations (1) exist to provide better health,
and (2) depend on consumer satisfaction, their view on whether
service is better. Few health care providers design services appropriately for the consumer. The organization that does will soon
provide services truly appreciated by its patients.

One of the best ways to help health care employees to see their
services from the patient's viewpoint is through training. Employees could be given training in such areas as "techniques in
serving patients," "listening to patients' problems and then solving
them," "turning patients' complaints into routine requests," and
"developing a consumer satisfaction approach in your department." Only after the entire staff—doctors, nurses, medical assis-
tants, administrators, nurses' aides, insurance clerks, financial coun-
selors, *everyone*—makes a commitment to be consumer oriented will
the organization actually realize an increase in consumer satisfaction.
Making such a commitment can also lead to higher morale among
the staff itself, as employees begin to feel more appreciated by their
satisfied customers (and as salaries increase to reflect the increase in
business).

SOME POINTS TO REMEMBER

- Everyone needs and deserves satisfactory health care services—these services are more available now than ever before.
- Health services would not be needed, without patients. Why
  don't health care providers more carefully consider patients'

(consumers') needs in the planning, delivery, and evaluation of services?

- National health insurance has been supported by many. If enacted, it will cover charges incurred by health care consumers, so that they may go just about anywhere to have their health needs met. Patients will eventually become very selective in seeking these services.
- Consumers have a tendency not to complain openly about problems or poor service. Instead, they will leave the doctors' office without informing anyone of their concerns, thus making it impossible to correct the problem. (Of course, the patient's business is lost, along with the business of everyone else who comes in contact with that patient.)
- Both positive and negative information about one's practice should be sought from patients. It is extremely helpful to obtain negative information, since problems (or just poor service) can be improved after being identified.
- One way to influence a consumer is to talk in terms of what he or she wants. Patients seem to be developing an ever-increasing attitude favoring "shopping for health care" and are willing to drive past locally available doctors if they believe better care is available at another location.
- Examine the system for delivering services. Focus attention on those needs determined by the patients to be important.
- Implement a consumer-oriented approach to health care with a focus on excellence in both care and service. Train members of your staff to become consumer oriented through voluntary commitment.
- Satisfied patients will inform others about quality service. Not only will new referrals increase but so will morale among your staff, because of the appreciation extended to them by these patients and because of increases in their salaries related to increased profits in the practice.

Chapter 3

Making Consumer Satisfaction a Way of Doing Business

The Service Isn't Right Until the Consumer Says So

ADOPTING A CONSUMERS' BILL OF RIGHTS

To thrive rather than just survive in today's competitive health care marketplace, every medical practice must acknowledge that the recipient of its services is a consumer, one whose rights must be observed. No matter how large or small a medical practice—whether it has one or more than a thousand physicians—it must embrace the opportunity of assuring each consumer the following rights.

Every Consumer Has the Right to High-Quality Health Care

- The consumer deserves health care of the highest quality that money can buy.
- The consumer deserves the kind of care that will enable him or her to live a long, productive life.

Every Consumer Has the Right to Long-Term Health Protection

- The consumer deserves the security of knowing that he or she is receiving the best possible return on investment for the dollars spent for health care.
- The consumer deserves to receive health care consistent with the high standards required by the Hippocratic Oath.

Every Consumer Has the Right to Friendly Evaluation and Competent Treatment

- The consumer deserves to be treated as a person in need of health services, not just as a checkbook.
- The consumer deserves to do business with health care providers who are interested in his or her needs, not just in the wants of the providers.

Every Consumer Has the Right to Information

- The consumer deserves to understand clearly the condition of his or her health and how to maintain and/or improve it.
- The consumer deserves to know the truth about the status of his or her health.

Every Consumer Has the Right to Address Grievances

- The consumer deserves to be heard. Physicians cannot be expected to be perfect in their interactions with patients, but an uncaring response to a patient's concern is inexcusable.
- Consumers deserve to have their concerns listened to and addressed by the health care professionals who serve them.

Every Consumer Has the Right to Satisfaction

- The consumer deserves more than just a "thank you."
- The consumer deserves excellent care and service in order to feel totally satisfied with the treatment he or she received. This includes feeling satisfied with a health care provider's attitude during treatment as well as with the quality of the care.

In other words, the consumer deserves:

- to receive care and service of high quality that the consumer perceives as excellent;
- to receive protection from unwarranted or improper care;
- to receive friendly and competent treatment;
- to know the truth about the status of his or her health;
- to be heard; and
- to feel totally satisfied with the care and treatment received— "excellence."

SUGGESTION BOX

For identifying and then following up on less than satisfactory service:

- Ask your consumers how satisfied they were with the services provided. You can do this in person, by telephone, or by mail, after the visit to the office.

- Invite groups of patients and/or their families to quarterly meetings to address complaints about less than satisfactory service and to offer suggestions that might help resolve the problems.

- Send a follow-up letter to each patient or the patient's family, after an evaluation or treatment, to let them know about the status of the patient's health, what needs to be done to improve it, and what questions need to be answered before further treatment can proceed.

- Provide educational opportunities for patients and their families. These could include classes or support groups where they could learn more about their particular medical concerns or conditions and possible courses of treatment.

- Provide friendly, helpful assistance with insurance claims and billing.

- Encourage patients to call you at your expense—toll-free or collect—with questions or concerns about their treatment plan or if they need help with insurance claims.

- Establish a definition of consumer satisfaction based upon excellence that acknowledges that the consumer's needs and desires are to be fulfilled concerning quality of both clinical care and service. Make sure everyone in the practice understands the meaning of consumer satisfaction and understands his or her role in implementing it through voluntary commitment.

- Ensure that consumers receive appropriate and timely information regarding the status of their health.

- Design a process that promotes a continuing relationship between physicians and consumers. For example, send out periodic newsletters, announcements of changes in staff, or notices of new programs or expanded hours to all consumers who use your medical facility.

- Promote consumer access to videotapes and libraries that provide medical information in lay terms.

- If practical, establish closed-circuit televised programming for consumers, so they can view special programs regarding their interests in health care.

- Draft a formal "Bill of Rights" for patients. This sets the stage for patients—and their families—to participate fully in their care and in follow-up treatment.

BECOMING CONSUMER ORIENTED

Health care is a competitive business and, as such, part of the free-enterprise system. Its product: care and service of high quality. The quality of care and service that a patient receives while under the treatment of a health care professional is what he or she will remember longest. It is also what will bring the patient back to the practice when further care is needed. Providers must therefore emphasize excellence in individualized, patient-oriented service to keep current patients, and to enjoy success in recruiting new ones.

Consumer satisfaction in the health care setting, can be measured objectively. Medical practices already measure, either by time or by function, the services they provide. These measurements can be found in fee schedules and other accounting practices. Consumer satisfaction with the care and quality of service can similarly be measured at each stage of delivery. For example, asking consumers to fill out a short questionnaire after a visit to your clinic or hospital can provide valuable tips on how to improve services. By encouraging patients' feedback on services and then acting on those suggestions, providers can give patients the opportunity to participate actively in planning their own health care.

Active participation by patients is the hallmark of a successful consumer satisfaction program. Once the patient believes that a health care professional is sincerely interested in his or her opinion about the care being received, a visible change in the patient's attitude can be seen. Patients become much more open about their feelings and concerns. Most important, this information then helps the attending physician or other health care provider to better meet the patient's medical needs. Patients and clinicians alike benefit from these partnerships: Patients receive care directly related to their individual needs, and providers watch their practices thrive and grow, as word gets around that they are patient oriented.

Without a strong partnership between those providing and those consuming health care, consumer satisfaction happens only randomly. Yet for too long, even in the most respected medical centers and physicians' offices, the patient's role in health care has been of secondary concern. Only recently have providers realized the importance of their voluntary commitment to attaining partnerships with their patients and of including them in their own care.

Tips for Becoming Service-Oriented

Remember that your medical practice is a competitive business; treat it accordingly.

Keep in mind that many patients consider the quality of care and service they receive to be as important as the end result.

Devise ways to measure the quality of service in your practice by establishing excellence criteria.

Build partnerships with your patients. Their perceptions and attitudes toward you will become more positive when they know that you value their opinions about the care they are receiving.

Remember that a patient-oriented health care practice grows and thrives.

RECOMMENDATIONS FOR MAKING CONSUMER SATISFACTION A WAY OF DOING BUSINESS

In your medical practice, you can make consumer satisfaction a way of doing business by (1) establishing excellence standards that define, measure, and monitor consumer satisfaction; (2) increasing support from and involvement of managers; (3) using tools to assure quality care and service; and (4) improving relations with patients, providers, and employees predicated upon mutual trust to work toward the achievement of excellence. The following are some recommendations.

Recommendation #1: Define Consumer Satisfaction

Adopt a definition of consumer satisfaction founded upon excellence that incorporates the views of physicians, employees, patients, and administrators.

A Sample Definition

Consumer satisfaction is the perception held by consumers inside and outside of the organization that their needs and desires concerning their health care have been fulfilled, and that they feel they received a high quality of both treatment and services, which they rate as excellent.

Defining the consumers of your medical practice is essential. Considerations should include:

- Patients
- Regulatory agencies
- Families of patients
- Physicians
- Contracting parties such as groups that use your lab, radiology, and consulting physicians
- Nonphysician staff
- Payers (government, HMOs, and other third parties)
- Other producers/users

Recommendation #2: Develop Written Surveys of Patient Satisfaction

The surveys can be mailed to patients either at or after their discharge from the hospital or completion of their treatment at the provider's office. Questions should cover such matters as the staff's concern for the patient, the quality and quantity of medical and nursing care, the quality of information supplied to the patient, the friendliness of the staff, the promptness of service, and prices and billing procedures. Be sure to encourage patients to sign the forms in your survey, to allow for follow-up calls to clarify areas of low satisfaction. You should also ask for demographic information and about any other needs they may have concerning health care.

Recommendation #3: Establish Focus Groups of Consumers

Invite five or six active patients and perhaps one member of each family to a meeting of a focus group, to discuss their perceptions of the service they received while at your medical practice. Be sure to provide all participants with a free lunch and parking. An experienced facilitator should lead the meeting, making sure that the patients feel comfortable in expressing their opinions about the quality of care and service. The facilitator should write a summary of positive and negative comments that emerge from the focus group.

These comments should then be organized according to department or service, and the complete summary sent to appropriate providers, administrators, and managers. To ensure that all points brought up in the meeting are thoroughly understood and acted upon, the meeting should be videotaped. Pertinent physicians and nonphysician staff should be encouraged to view the video, and it should be discussed at departmental meetings. The confidentiality of testimonies from patients, of course, should always be honored.

Recommendation #4: Place Consumer Satisfaction on the Agenda for Planning Meetings

Both physicians and managers need to make consumer satisfaction the way of doing business. Thus, consumer satisfaction should be discussed as an item on the agenda at joint planning meetings for your hospital and medical clinic. It should be directly included in all plans for the medical practice.

Recommendation #5: Encourage Top Physicians and Managers to Have Direct Contact with Patients

All members of top management should introduce themselves to at least one consumer each week and ask about his or her visit to the medical practice. Top management should also take turns assisting staff in areas where large numbers of patients wait for service. They should wear their name tags at these sites, so that patients can clearly identify them.

Recommendation #6: Make Consumer Satisfaction Part of all Evaluations of Employee Performance

Standards for consumer satisfaction should be incorporated into all evaluations of employee performance, including those for physicians. Such standards should be part of the guidelines for the office, practice, company handbooks, and personnel policies for the organization.

Recommendation #7: Make Consumer Satisfaction a Routine Subject for Discussion at Meetings of Your Office or Department

Physicians and managers should clarify the priority given to consumer satisfaction within the medical practice. Nurses and physicians should provide input, feedback, and follow-up. Routine reports on progress in resolving identified problems with consumer satisfaction should be scheduled at subsequent meetings, thus implementing continuous quality enhancement.

Recommendation #8: Train Head Nurses and Physicians in Management and in Interpersonal and Communicative Skills

Top management must see to it that nurses and physicians are provided with the necessary education and training that will ensure consumer satisfaction through excellence in care and service.

Recommendation #9: Solicit Opinions from Employees

Employees should be asked for their perceptions about the working environment and problems in performance of services.

Recommendation #10: Recognize "Heroes" in Quality of Care and Service with Dramatic Awards

To provide a meaningful incentive to change behavior, award employees with days off, vacation, or cash bonuses for their efforts in improving consumer satisfaction. Name a "Pro of the Month." Employees should be "caught being good" and rewarded for it!

Recommendation #11: Make Criteria for Performance in Consumer Satisfaction Part of Every Employee's Job Description

These criteria should also be a substantial part of performance reviews and considerations for raises in pay, for all staff and employees.

Recommendation #12: Tailor Training Sessions in Consumer Satisfaction Specifically to Each Service Unit and/or Department

Although all employees should receive such training, the sessions should focus on employees in positions with high levels of public contact, such as physicians, nurses, receptionists, and patient account representatives. Participation in training is a requirement. The performance of these skills should be included in annual performance reviews. Physicians, nurses, chief technicians, and/or departmental managers should be trained first, so that they can demonstrate leadership by example.

Recommendation #13: Implement a Formal Program of Patient Education

Through a formal program for patient education, both patients and their families can receive information about their condition and about options for its treatment. Special classes on common medical conditions and treatment should also be made available to all health care consumers. Personal letters should be sent to all patients following treatment. The letters should explain what happened during the visit, answer all questions that might have arisen from the visit, and restate instructions given to the patient regarding their self care with or without medication or therapy.

Recommendation #14: Provide Patients with Assistance in Processing Bills and Insurance Claims

Designate a person from the billing or insurance department to be available to answer questions from patients and their families. Distribute to patients a telephone number where they can get quick and easy answers to their questions. Many medical practices have an 800 number for this purpose.

Recommendation #15: Develop Scheduling Procedures That Recognize and Value Each Patient's Time

Identify scheduling procedures that would maximize physicians' time, yet not inconvenience patients. Develop schedules to meet patient needs; for instance, before or after work, off hours, and weekends.

Chapter 4

Developing
Consumer-Oriented Service

THE PHYSICIAN'S ROLE IN DEVELOPING
A CONSUMER-ORIENTED INITIATIVE

Physicians must now take steps, through voluntary commitment, to improve the quality of service they provide their customers. Because of the physician-oriented nature of the health care marketplace, it is up to physicians to take leadership positions in this effort. Such an initiative should be:

1. integrated with current programs for improving quality care and service, managing risk, and managing care;
2. consumer driven, with leadership by physicians; and
3. designed as an ongoing process that will result in fundamental operational changes to achieve and maintain excellence.

The initiative must improve the quality of service in ways consistent with other key factors for success: quality of medical care and cost effectiveness.

When a program for consumer satisfaction is initiated, discrepancies can be anticipated between leadership goals for the program and physicians' acceptance of those goals. Physicians are usually more focused on patient outcomes, while administrators typically emphasize the process of delivery. Medical and administrative goals can be integrated, however, by having the two groups work together in the planning and implementation of the program. Issues that are likely to emerge between physicians and administrators about consumer satisfaction include:

- lack of information regarding the necessity for its development and implementation;
- lack of incentives;
- lack of agreement on its meaning; and
- lack of agreement on its business value.

Physicians must be specifically addressed on the merits of incorporating consumer satisfaction into the conduct of their practices. Most physicians do not receive any formal training on this subject during medical school, residency, or experiences in fellowships. The process of persuading physicians to accept this idea begins with education. Here are some recommendations:

Recommendation #1: Get Physicians to Take Leadership in the Establishment of a Consumer Satisfaction Program Through Voluntary Commitment Aimed at Excellence in Care and Service

Historically, the practice of medicine has been "physician driven" although, in response to cost-containment measures in recent health care reforms, nonphysician medical professionals or providers are increasingly being used to deliver certain medical services. Yet only physicians can admit patients to a hospital, and only physicians—or their appropriate designees—can prescribe regulated medications. For a system of consumer satisfaction to work, therefore, it must be physician driven or led. Physicians must voluntarily commit to establishing a consumer satisfaction program and, by their own example, set the standards of care and service for others in the practice to follow. Top management support is, however, necessary for physicians to take such a lead. It allows physicians to focus on physician-to-physician communication about consumer satisfaction, an essential element in making any program work.

Recommendation #2: Educate Physicians by Demonstrating the Importance of Consumer Satisfaction to the Successful Operation of a Medical Practice

The long-term economic success of a medical practice rests on a steady or slightly increasing number of patients. Due to the current trend of decreasing reimbursement from third-party payers, it has become more difficult to obtain revenues in excess of expenses without significantly increasing the number of paying consumers. This situation is currently being tested under the "capitation system," in which managed care plans pay providers a set amount for giving care to a certain number of patients. If providers find they need to spend more than that amount to take care of their designated patients, they will have to do so out of their own pockets. Thus, under the capitation system, providers must be able to attract and keep as many healthy patients as possible, to balance the financial impact of those who need more care.

A practice built on consumer satisfaction is assured of return appointments. Satisfied patients and their families also bring in new patients through word-of-mouth testimonials. Physicians, however, have been taught in their medical training that to satisfy consumers, all they need to do is provide competent patient care. Thus, they do not feel a need to be educated about consumer satisfaction—something they think they are already providing. Research shows otherwise. Studies have revealed that no significant connection exists between patient satisfaction and physicians' *perception* of it.

Physicians must therefore be educated on the importance of patient/physician interactions and on how such interactions relate directly to the economic success of their practice. Studies have found that the conduct of a physician, as perceived by patients and their families, is clearly the most important factor determining whether or not consumers feel satisfied with the care they have received. Other factors—accessibility, availability of other specialists, completeness of the facilities, and continuity of care—also contribute to consumer satisfaction, but not as much as the conduct of the physician. In one study that looked at why families change pediatricians, the determining factors that parents cited concerning their satisfaction with a particular pediatrician's care were all related to the personal qualities of the physician—his or her communication skills, clinical competence, and apparent level of concern for the child. Parents said that dissatisfaction with the "structural" features of a medical facility—costs, waiting time, and continuity with the same physician—were less likely to make them change pediatricians than was dissatisfaction with the personal attitude and demeanor of the physician during treatment.

Recommendation #3: Incorporate Standards for Consumer Satisfaction into Evaluations of Each Provider's Performance

Responses from surveys of patient satisfaction should be included in each physician's performance evaluation—right along with indicators of the physician's productivity and ability to meet his or her staff obligations. Some medical groups encourage the involvement of physicians in community service and activities in volunteer organizations such as serving as the physician for a high school's athletic team or working for charitable organizations. Such outside involvement demonstrates interest in the community and is often considered by committees on compensation when they evaluate salary adjustments.

Surveys of patient satisfaction can be coded by specialty, by program, or by individual physician. The surveys would thus become a database for evaluating the performance of each physician. Once the first set of results has been collected and analyzed, they become a baseline measure from which subsequent measurements can be made to determine whether any progress has been made toward correcting less than favorable results.

Recommendation #4: Provide Head Nurses and Physicians with Education and Hands-On Training in Management and Budgeting, As Well As Interpersonal and Communication Skills

A broadened awareness of and involvement in the management of a medical practice will increase the probability that a physician will embrace a consumer-oriented approach to doing business. Each member of the medical and supporting staffs needs to have a stake in the management of consumer satisfaction. A team approach to the issue will have a greater impact on the achievement of excellence in consumer satisfaction than will one or more members of the staff acting as individuals.

Recommendation #5: Measure Physician Satisfaction Through Anonymous Questionnaires for Employees

If physicians are not satisfied with their working environment, it is unlikely that their supporting staff or their patients will be pleased, either. Harmony—and disharmony—are contagious. It is therefore important to identify and rectify less than harmonious relationships among staff before their negative side effects detract from the quality of care and services being offered consumers. Employees, including physicians, should be given questionnaires periodically to find out what they like or do not like about their working environment. Areas of dissatisfaction should be discussed at medical staff meetings, and appropriate solutions or responses should be developed to increase physician satisfaction. Other steps that can be taken include:

- telling physicians whenever positive and negative comments about their care appear in the surveys of patient satisfaction;
- decreasing patients' rate of "no-shows" by instructing ancillary staff to make reminding telephone calls to patients twenty-four hours before their scheduled appointments; and
- fostering good relationships between physicians and supporting staff by planning shared lunches, parties, and other get-togethers.

Recommendation #6: Reward Behavior by Providers and Support Staff That Demonstrates Competence, Caring, and Good Use of Communication Skills

Develop a special award such as "Pro of the Month," or other ways of recognizing providers and support staff for excellence in service to consumers. The Pro of the Month could be chosen from the entire pool of employees, or from separate groups for physicians and for other employees. Each year, award the provider who received the most positive responses in the patient satisfaction surveys with a meaningful memento such as a gold pin, a pen, a trophy, or a desk ornament. Develop a system of monetary rewards for providers who exhibit excellence in consumer satisfaction. The system should be linked to basic compensation or to incentive/bonus pay.

Recommendation #7: Give Providers Ongoing Information About How to Continue the Emphasis on Consumer-Oriented Service

The results of each survey should routinely be shared with physicians and their supporting teams. Past performance should be compared to current trends to determine the effects of any changes that have been made to improve less than satisfactory services. This is the time to refocus efforts and to emphasize the changes called for by consumers. Successful strategies would include:

- providing, for viewing at medical staff meetings, videos of patients' focus groups in which patients are shown discussing problems and suggesting changes;
- involving physicians in activities for marketing and public relations—those aimed at referring physicians as well as at patients; and
- offering seminars for physicians on the topic of enhancing consumer satisfaction, led by outside consultants, and making the concept of consumer satisfaction part of the orientation of physicians new to the practice.

HOW CONSUMERS SELECT AND EVALUATE PHYSICIANS

To develop an effective marketing message for their practice, health care providers must first understand the factors and criteria consumers use when selecting and evaluating their physicians. In

March 1987, Ramsey Clinic hired Nelson Research Services, Inc., to conduct a study of how people living in the area served by the clinic select their primary physicians. A scientific sample of 240 people were interviewed for the study, some in person, others on the telephone. Findings of the study offer some important information about consumers and the factors they consider when selecting their physicians. Here is a summary of the findings of that study[1]:

- Three-fourths of consumers in the five-county area served by Ramsey Clinic have a personal physician. People living in rural areas, women, and people sixty years of age or older were more likely to have a personal physician, while men in general and adults under thirty were less likely.
- Most primary care physicians are general practitioners. Very few specialists (other than family practitioners and internists) function as primary care physicians.

About three of every ten consumers in the five county area have been with their current primary care physicians for at least ten years. Long-term relationships with physicians are especially common in rural areas and among consumers sixty years of age or older. This suggests that these rural and older consumers are least likely to switch to a different primary care physician.

The most important factors to consumers when choosing a primary care physician are all related to the interpersonal skills of the physician and his or her staff. In this survey, consumers cited the following specific factors as being most important:

- The physician's skill at communicating—at listening, asking questions, and explaining medical matters in understandable language
- The physician's diagnostic and problem-solving skills
- The physician's willingness to refer the patient to another physician for services in a specialty or perhaps for a second opinion

- The physician's ability to project a kind, caring, and considerate manner to the patient
- The physician's willingness to involve the patient in making decisions about treatment and care
- The physician's availability for consultations by telephone
- The attitude and manner of the physician's staff

On the other hand, many factors played little or no role in selection or evaluation of a primary care physician by a consumer. These included:

- The physician's gender, age, and mode of dress
- The medical school the physician attended
- The physician's affiliation with a teaching or research facility
- The size of the medical group
- Whether the patient was referred to the physician by a referral service
- The availability of parking at the physician's office or clinic
- The physician's fees

Several other factors fell somewhere in the middle. They were of some importance to consumers when selecting a physician. These include (in order of importance):

- Length of lead time required to schedule an appointment with the physician
- Whether the physician expressed a friendly interest in the patient, beyond his or her immediate health problems
- Length of time spent in a waiting room (most consumers judge a twenty-minute wait acceptable, although men, consumers in upper-income brackets, and residents of the metropolitan area are less patient than others—but all consumers are agreeable to waiting longer than twenty minutes if given a good reason)
- The reputation of the clinic
- The location of the office or clinic
- The physician's previous working experience

- The physician's practice of offering follow-up by letter or telephone
- The availability in the clinic of a wide variety of specialists
- The hours the clinic is open
- The physician's affiliation with a large group of specialists
- Recommendation of the physician by a friend

Interestingly, the overall ranking of factors used to pick a primary care physician was similar for all segments of people surveyed, regardless of area (rural or metropolitan), gender, age, income, or insurance coverage.

From another perspective, analyses of findings of this study place health care consumers in the area served by Ramsey Clinic in three basic categories:

1. Consumers to whom interpersonal skills are key factors in choosing and evaluating a physician; 89 percent fall into this group.
2. Consumers who are practical, oriented to convenience, and choose their physicians accordingly; 8 percent do this.
3. Consumers who assign a high value to technical considerations; only 2 percent of consumers are of this type.

Therefore, the technical competence that distinguishes Ramsey Clinic from its competition—its affiliation with a teaching and research facility, and its expansive multispecialty network of physicians—influences only 2 percent of people in the area served by the clinic when it comes time to choose medical care (see Table 4.1). Furthermore, it is important to note that respondents to the survey indicated that they do not consider it particularly difficult to find physicians who offer the benefits they are looking for. This finding emphasizes how intensely competitive the health care industry has become in this five-county metropolitan area.

Blue Cross and Blue Shield of Minnesota (BCBSM), divides its members with recommendations on the type of questions to ask potential providers.[2] Overall, BCBSM advocates that you should have a doctor with whom you can freely discuss each health issue. Listening to each question and taking the required time to explain all answers is essential.

TABLE 4.1. Factors Considered by Consumers When Selecting a Physician

Major Factors	Principal Components
Personal relationships	Willing to talk on telephone Good communicative skills Involves patient in decisions Spends time, doesn't rush Kind, considerate, caring Willing to refer patient Letter/phone follow-up
Convenience	Time spent in waiting room
Practicality	Length of time to schedule an appointment Hours Physician's fee Availability of parking Location
Technical	Affiliation with a teaching facility Affiliation with a research facility Physician's medical school Size of group (number of physicians) Referred by referral service Affiliated with large group of specialists Clinic has physicians with wide range of ages

Source: Nelson, A. Consumer Satisfaction Evaluation Study of Ramsey Clinic Services. Internal study conducted by Nelson Research Services, Inc., Minneapolis/St. Paul, Minnesota, 1987. Reprinted by permission.

When you contact the medical group, ask to speak to a patient adviser or appointment coordinator who has been with the medical organization long enough to know how to answer your questions. Above all else, you must feel comfortable asking your doctor-to-be any health-related question that is important to you.

Specific questions in the selection process should include:

- What type (family practice, pediatrics, internal medicine, etc.) is available to address the particular health issue?
- Ask for an identification of the following:
  — Hospitals used if admission is required.
  — Specialists used if referral is necessary.

— Communication method and time line for receiving test results and treatment plan.
— Who bills the insurance company?
— Is a patient advocate available to help if needed?
— Office locations.
— Office hours. (What about evenings and weekends?)
— Arrangements for after-hours nonemergency care. (Ask about availability of a telephone, e-mail, or Internet number to call for general medical or other health-related advice.)
— Is there a toll-free telephone number for making appointments and calling with questions after the office visit?
— Average length of time to get the type of appointment needed.
— Any discount arrangements with area pharmacies?
— Will a follow-up summary report of results be sent to the patient after each visit?

THE ROLE OF MANAGEMENT IN DEVELOPING A CONSUMER-ORIENTED INITIATIVE

The implementation of a program for consumer satisfaction will typically encounter some roadblocks among the nonphysician staff as well as the physicians. Although top management is usually highly supportive of the concept, clinicians and members of the supporting and ancillary staffs frequently have had no consistent experience in making consumer satisfaction part of their day-to-day job performance. Furthermore, they are likely to perceive consumer satisfaction as a separate, compartmentalized function of the medical practice rather than as an integral aspect of each member's job.

Many factors appear to be responsible for these misconceptions. Consumer satisfaction may not have been made a priority within the practice. The practice may also lack clear guidelines and expectations for employee performance. A systematic procedure for rewarding excellence in consumer service also may not be in place. So how can the leadership of a medical practice persuade its clinicians and supporting staff to participate actively through voluntary commitment, to support and implement effectively, a program for consumer satisfaction? The following are some recommendations.

Recommendation #1: Develop a Practice-Oriented Mission Statement That Clearly Defines Excellent Care and Service As Essential to Long-Term Success, Then Develop an Organization-Wide Communication Plan to Reinforce It

A clear, concise, and highly visible mission statement communicates a strong and focused message to employees as well as to consumers. Through such a statement, both groups will have an improved understanding of the expectations of the organization regarding excellence in care and service. A strong mission statement also becomes a guiding light for the organization, defining the culture of the practice. The revision of a mission statement is, ultimately, the responsibility of the partners in the practice, its shareholders, or its board of directors. Top management, however, can assist this process, ensuring that the concept of excellence in care and service to consumers becomes a clear and concise element of the statement.

After the statement is revised, the next challenge is to increase its visibility. One way of doing this is to publicize the mission statement itself. Posters can be placed at strategic locations throughout the organization. The statement can also be included on the letterhead and prominently featured on all the brochures and publications.

To further increase the visibility of the mission statement—and the concept of consumer satisfaction as a way of doing business—a promotional campaign can be initiated within the organization. The campaign should have a theme or promotional slogan developed as an outgrowth of the statement, such as "You're Special at the Doctor's Clinic." The slogan could then be promoted through posters and publications. It could even be embossed on buttons worn by employees or included on their name tags.

The revised mission statement, the organizational emphasis on consumer satisfaction, and the promotional campaign can be presented to employees through a series of in-service programs. For these programs to be effective, all employees must be involved, no matter how much actual contact they have with patients. Employees must understand that it is important to treat each other, as well as patients, as consumers. Poor relationships among employees of an organization will spill over, with negative consequences, onto the relationships among employees and consumers. Be sure that all physicians and nonphysician management take part in the in-service programs; their presence lends credibility to the endeavor and provides evidence of top management support. But to avoid the perception of criticism, it is important to communicate to the rest of the staff that they are already doing a good job. They must also stress the importance of incorporating the principle of consumer satisfaction into the very fabric of the medical practice.

Recommendation #2: Develop or Revise Job Descriptions for Nonphysicians to State Clearly the Expectation That Employees Will Incorporate the Concept of High-Quality Care and Service and Consumer Satisfaction into Their Day-to-Day Job Performance

Job descriptions in a medical practice typically emphasize the clinical aspects of care, almost to the exclusion of everything else. Descriptions should be revised to include expectations concerning care and service to consumers. To permit quantitative evaluation, these expectations should be specifically defined and stated in measurable terms. In addition, programs for employee orientation should routinely devote time to the subject of consumer satisfaction. An employee's initial orientation should also be regularly followed up with continuing on-the-job training that reinforces and updates concepts and techniques. Once performance standards have been established, supervisory and rank-and-file employees can more appropriately work in concert to achieve excellence.

To consistently incorporate the concept of high-quality service to consumers—as well as other aspects of the mission statement—into day-to-day performance on the job, the organization should clearly outline its expectations of each employee in each job described. Rather than serving as a tool for pointing out poor performance, the job description should provide clear expectations of performance. It serves, therefore, as an instructional device and should specify the behaviors it expects of the employee, as concretely as possible. Those behaviors deemed necessary for an employee to enhance consumer satisfaction must be identified, prioritized, and incorporated into all job descriptions for the organization. A focus group of supervisory and nonsupervisory personnel could be formed, to get this process started. The objective for such a group should be to specify at least three measurable key behaviors for each job classification.

For a receptionist, for example, the key behaviors could include the following:

1. Answers the phone in three to five rings, using proper identification of the organization, the department, and his or her name
2. Acknowledges a patient's presence promptly with eye contact, a courteous hello, or if on the phone, some nonverbal signal such as a nod or a smile
3. Gives the patient undivided attention and uses effective communication techniques—empathy, confirming information, eye contact—to allow the patient to express his or her concerns or questions
4. Returns to calls on hold within thirty to sixty seconds while assuring waiting patients of continued attention to their needs

Recommendation #3: Use the Criteria of Consumer Satisfaction in Evaluations of Job Performance

Key indicators developed for job descriptions can be incorporated into evaluations of performance. This sets the stage for open dialogue between employee and supervisor concerning the concept of consumer satisfaction and how its measurable aspects will be considered in performance reviews. The employee receives important feedback concerning definable outcomes in this area, while the supervisor reemphasizes that consumer satisfaction remains a top priority for the organization. The performance evaluation also enables supervisors to identify substandard performance and to develop individual plans of action to correct the situation. Routine, ongoing monitoring of outcomes related to the plan for action enables employee and employer to chart results that will form bases for the next evaluation.

Recommendation #4: Develop a Pro of the Month Award, to Recognize Employees for Outstanding Performance in "Living the Mission Statement"

Programs for recognition of employees, such as a Pro of the Month award, are based on the proactive concept of "let's catch the employees doing it right." As noted in the section for physicians, Pro of the Month can include both physicians and nonphysicians, or a separate monthly designation can be made for each group. The award sends a clear message throughout the organization that efforts by employees are highly valued. As part of the award, the employee should receive personal notification by leaders of the organization, special recognition in the form of flowers and perhaps a lunch or dinner with the leaders, prominent coverage in in-house newsletters and on posters located in common areas throughout the organization, and the addition of the employee's name to a plaque honoring Pros of the Month in a central corridor of the organization. The award should provide recognition that is positive and highly visible. The committee selecting for these awards to both physicians and nonphysicians should be presented as a recognizable and respected group of physicians and nonphysicians. The purpose of the selecting committee is to establish the standards for qualification and then to solicit recommendations and applications for nominations each month, from the staff at large, and then select the most worthy member of the staff from among those nominated.

The Pro of the Month award offers a systematic and positive way of reinforcing the mission of the organization to provide outstanding service to consumers. Thus, criteria for the award should clearly correspond to the mission statement. The award should send a non-ambiguous message to all employees and to the community that the recipient of the reward is being acclaimed for "living the mission statement" of the practice.

Recommendation #5: Routinely Monitor the Results of Consumer Satisfaction Surveys

Routinely administered surveys provide a basis for monitoring the quantitative effectiveness of the program for consumer satisfaction. The surveys should be longitudinally charted to assure that the program is doing what it was designed to do. When measuring outcomes, it is most important to focus on less than satisfactory performance. Although it is also important to acknowledge and reward employees for what is going right, it is extremely important to identify and correct less than satisfactory services. Routine review of the outcomes will identify the elements responsible for the problems that necessitate changes leading to an improvement of the care or service activities in question. Each plan for remediation that is implemented to correct a problem with a care or service unit must be closely monitored to ensure the desired outcome.

THE ROLE OF NONPHYSICIAN STAFF IN MAKING A CONSUMER-ORIENTED INITIATIVE WORK

The top management of most medical practices is usually aware that a high level of consumer satisfaction is necessary for continued success. In some cases, however, leaders who recognize the importance of high-quality care and service find themselves working with a staff who have not yet experienced the same recognition. Consumer satisfaction has not yet become the way of doing business in those practices. It has not yet become part of the culture of that organization.

Difficulty in communicating about consumer satisfaction can be traced to two basic causes: (1) the widely diverse training and experience among individuals within a typical practice; and (2) problems related to the structure of a medical practice. Here are some recommendations for overcoming those difficulties and making consumer satisfaction part of the culture of the practice.

Recommendation #1: Treat Physicians and Nonphysician Staff As Consumers

Experts say that cultural acceptance is essential for the successful implementation of any major initiative in an organization. Using education to develop that culture is not enough. Change in organizational values must also occur. It begins by reinforcing a voluntary commitment to excellence by all medical staff and employees.

One way of initiating change in organizational values is to expand the traditional definition of "consumer" to include fellow physicians and nonphysician staff. Satisfying these "internal customers" should be given the same priority as satisfying external ones, and it should occur on both the interpersonal and the interdepartmental levels. The manner in which one member of the staff treats another is contagious; it will influence how the staff treats patients and other outside customers. As one management expert has suggested, "the employee's capacity to provide quality service to other employees and customers will be directly related to the quality of service they receive as internal customers of the organization's day-to-day management."[3] Thus, by improving employee satisfaction, an organization will be likely to see improvements in patient satisfaction as well.

Both physicians and other leaders must become role models for the "ethic of excellence in consumer satisfaction." Managers may have little contact with external customers on a day-to-day basis, but they have many opportunities to show exemplary consumer-oriented behavior in their service to each other and to those they supervise, which they can demonstrate by "walking their talk." In fact, administrative job descriptions and incentive plans should be modified to include criteria that measure the level of consumer satisfaction they provide to "intraorganizational consumers," or other employees. Criteria should be included that measure how well they provide to the employees they supervise a role model for the ethic of excellence in consumer satisfaction. Leadership through voluntary commitment is the key to initiating cultural change within organizations.

Recommendation #2: Change Organizational Values That Hinder the Successful Implementation of a Program for Consumer Satisfaction

The most important element of any attempt to make an organizational change is ensuring that the change becomes so internalized and so much a part of the everyday workings of the organization that it will last long after the initial incentives to implement the change have gone. Consumer satisfaction must become a way business is routinely conducted in the health care industry. Changing organizational norms is, however, extremely difficult. Kilmann suggests the following approach:[4]

1. Work with groups of employees to elicit lists of the norms of the practice—both positive and negative (e.g., tardiness, working through lunch, absenteeism, going the extra mile, etc.). This process is designed to allow employees to see the counterproductive "directives" they have imposed on one another.
2. Work with staff to establish new norms. This step in the process should include discussion of where the organization is headed—its mission, vision, core values, goals, and objectives. From these discussions, employees should be able to develop an acceptable list of norms that fit with the goals of the organization. The following have been documented as values often found among employees working in organizations with a commitment to service:[5]

   • Respect for each other
   • Friendly work environment
   • Acknowledgment of the service mission
   • Universal accountability for behavior—everyone is expected to obey the rules
   • Participation in decision making and discussion
   • Teamwork
   • Excellent care and service to consumers

3. Identify gaps between existing norms in the practice and the new, desired norms.
4. Close the gaps. Having a list of new organizational values is not enough. Those values must be put into practice. This can be accomplished in a variety of ways. Some of the most important include:

   • role modeling by physicians and nonphysicians;
   • clear communication of values through changes in job descriptions and mission statements; and
   • ceremonies to award recognition upon reaching important predefined milestones.

Including members of the staff as active participants in defining the new norms will create the staff ownership needed to implement change. Staff members will be more likely to encourage each other to adhere to the new values and let go of the old.

Recommendation #3: Implement the Program for Consumer Satisfaction on a Service-by-Service Basis; Also, Work to Create a Model Program That Can Serve As an Example for Others

Individual leaders among physicians and nonphysician staff should be made responsible for implementing the program in their own services. This recognizes that different services make changes at different rates. It will also allow leaders to focus on specific problems related to each of their services. The creation of a model service provides an example for other services to emulate and a chance for managers to demonstrate the benefits of a consumer satisfaction program. Using members of the staff from that service as trainers for other services will facilitate expansion of the program throughout the organization. They will have become the experts and will appear credible when training people to do the same jobs they do themselves. Appropriate recognition should be given as each service reaches designated milestones in the implementation of their satisfaction program.

Recommendation #4: Hold Educational Seminars on the Subject of Consumer Satisfaction and Include the Topic as Part of Other Presentations on Service in Health Care Delivery

The goal of the educational process should be to inform staff of progress made toward the attainment of goals and objectives in consumer satisfaction, and of ways this information is related to care and service to the medical practice. Ideas that have proven beneficial for certain services should be discussed and adapted for implementation by other providers. The following are some general suggestions for which specific examples could be drawn and presented at educational sessions:[6]

- Point out that to survive, the practice must attract consumers and that a high level of consumer satisfaction is one way of doing that. Show the correlation between the number of returning visits made by patients, and their levels of satisfaction.
- Point out that consumer satisfaction is the lifeblood of most service industries. Excellent service motivates us to shop at certain stores; why shouldn't it motivate us when selecting the place where we receive our health care? Show examples where low levels of patient satisfaction led to an erosion of the patient base and poor morale among the physician and non-physician staff.
- Stress that satisfaction can make the medical practice a better place to work. A program for consumer satisfaction has very good potential to improve employee satisfaction on the job, once the staff begin to treat each other as they would like to be treated themselves.
- Note that it is already working. Allow past Pros of the Month and other employees who are pleased with the program to give testimonials and teach others about its merits.
- Show clips of taped comments, both critical and complimentary, from consumer focus groups. These should illustrate the significance consumers place on such things as having providers courteously answer each patient's questions, having the staff answer phone calls promptly, and getting friendly help with questions about billing. Results from past and current surveys should be discussed, to demonstrate quantifiable outcomes and to associate key findings with patient activity and financial benchmarks.

Recommendation #5: Expand the Definition of "Consumer" to Include Employees As Well As Patients

Staff should be taught to serve internal consumers—fellow employees—with the same commitment as when serving external consumers. Studies confirm the positive, contagious nature of treating others as you would like to be treated yourself. Once in motion, this aspect of behavior will be shared with all people with whom an employee comes in contact—staff and patients alike. Furthermore, such commitment should be recognized; staff should have a uniform way of rewarding those within the organization who serve each other well. Employees of Federal Express, for example, use special stickers that can be placed on memos or paperwork to recognize those who serve them well or who are doing a good job in general. Many for-profit companies reward employees with financial incentives, knowing that investment comes back to the owners as return business.

Recommendation #6: Develop a Survey of Satisfaction Among the Staff

These should be similar to the surveys of satisfaction used among patients and other external consumers. Through these internal surveys, job satisfaction and service relationships within the organization can be measured and evaluated. The results of these surveys should also be used in evaluations of employee performance and for setting new goals for care and service.

Recommendation #7: Modify Administrative and Managerial Job Descriptions and Performance Evaluations to Include Criteria on Consumer Satisfaction and Support with Compensation

The criteria should be based on service to those whom managers supervise (internal consumers) as well as on their service to patients. Administrators should be evaluated for how well they serve as a role model for the ethic of excellence in consumer satisfaction. Top management should review the program for consumer satisfaction at regular intervals. Routine review, at least annually, is required to make sure the program remains on course and is still applicable. Compensation will reinforce the desired behavior. Rewarded activity is continuously repeated. Employee feedback from surveys should prove a useful tool in evaluating the program.

Chapter 5

From Initial Call for Appointment to Billing: Treating the Patient Right

When patients arrive at a hospital or a physician's office, they are there for help. Whether they are merely seeking information about a new insurance plan or checking in for gallbladder surgery, they have come for one reason: to get assistance with a problem. The quickest way to create dissatisfied patients is to treat them poorly during this initial contact, but unfortunately it is done all too often. Instead of showing an interest in patients' needs, medical facilities usually insist that patients deal first with the bureaucratic demands of the organization—asking them, for example, to fill out forms, or to first check in at the desk that handles insurance, to make sure the bill will be paid, or embarrassing them by indicating they are too early or too late for their appointment.

BEFORE THE APPOINTMENT

In anticipation of a patient's visit, whether to a doctor's office or a hospital, several considerations are important to make the visit satisfying and efficient. For some patients, it may be advantageous to schedule all appointments on the same day, ending with a staff meeting to summarize all findings. Other patients, to avoid exhaustion, may appreciate appointments coordinated over more than one day. In the past, many specialists accepted referrals only from other physicians, but most medical practices today are quite open to accepting appointments for patients who have demonstrated insurability, whether or not they were directly referred by another physician. It should be pointed out, however, that most plans from a HMO will limit and/or direct their referrals to specialists and will almost always permit such referrals only after the patient has been evaluated by a primary care physician seen by the HMO as a "gatekeeper."

Many patients find it helpful to receive written brochures or other literature describing a particular program or service at a hospital or clinic. Such information can provide a background and, in many cases, can help set the patient and family at ease about going to a doctor whom they have never met before.

Service on questions of fees, insurance, and financial needs should be brought up, as the plan for evaluating satisfaction is developed. Too frequently, patients are not given clear answers to their questions about costs and, as a result, remain unaware of the financial impact of their care until a bill is received. As patients are responsible for paying their bills, they should know approximately how much the charges are going to be before treatment begins. If the patient has insurance, staff should help verify the extent of their coverage prior to the service; every insurance policy is different, and the cost to be covered by the patient may vary considerably. This may require that the staff do some searching and perhaps telephoning to secure the information—but such duties are required of a consumer-oriented business. Patients who appear embarrassed about paying their bills should be quickly befriended by the staff, and an effort should be made to find out what outside financial resources might be available. Many health care providers should consider setting up an installment plan based on ability to pay, for low-income patients.

ESTABLISHING RAPPORT

If patients are treated poorly during the first few minutes after their arrival at a medical practice, chances are quite good they will not return. A more appropriate way of greeting newly arrived patients is to smile and welcome them into the setting with a cheerful "hello" or "good afternoon." Such common pleasantries establish a friendly and informal, yet businesslike, attitude. Staff should also be encouraged to offer a kind compliment or two to the patient, if appropriate, on what he or she is wearing, or perhaps to make a comment about the weather or about parking difficulties. Such personalized pleasantries are easy to make and will help patients relax and feel that the staff is interested in them as people, rather than just "health cases."

Members of the staff should identify themselves to the patient by name, and briefly indicate who they are (nurse, doctor, receptionist). They should then describe to the patient how they plan to help. Here are two examples of beginnings for such a dialogue:

> Hello. My name is Sally Jones. I am a patient coordinator, and I am here to help you today. Do you have any questions, before we begin? First, I would like to outline what you can expect to happen at each of your appointments.

> Good morning. I am Doctor Smith. I am a pediatrician. My special training is in pediatric cardiology, and I will be giving your son a physical examination. This examination will be used to determine whether it will be necessary to do additional testing of his heart. My procedure will involve . . .

This open and easygoing communicative pattern between the patient and staff members should continue throughout the appointment. Each dialogue sets in motion a clear, meaningful relationship with the patient. Briefly outlining what will be taking place during the appointment allows the patient to prepare, both physically and mentally, for what will follow.

DEFINING THE PATIENT'S NEEDS AND WANTS

Always talk in terms of what the patient wants. In a friendly way, convince the patient that you are going to do everything reasonably possible to make sure his or her needs are met, but that to accomplish this, you must have the patient's total, undivided cooperation. Ask yourself, "How can I encourage them to want to do it?" Demanding cooperation seldom works. Rather, you must plan an approach that encourages patients to see that their needs can best be met by cooperating with you.

When confronted with an uncooperative patient, it is natural to recoil with defensiveness. All members of the staff must learn, however, that they must exert as much willpower as necessary to resist responding with the same kind of abrasiveness. The only way to come out ahead, in an argument, is to avoid the argument in the first place. So even if the patient is clearly wrong, avoid debating the point. One argument may lead to another, creating an even more uncooperative patient.

You also have the patient's health to consider. Arguing with patients who are ill, especially those with dangerously high blood pressure or other serious conditions, might exacerbate their health problems. Remember Murphy's Law: "Anything that can go wrong, will go wrong." So, instead of arguing, concede to the patient that you are wrong. It will do absolutely no good to lose control of your temper. A patient who believes he or she has been neglected or mistreated will never be won over by an out-of-control argument.

Instead of reacting defensively, train yourself to let the "hot air go in one ear and out the other," and listen for a comment from the patient or a pause in the conversation that you can use to find common ground. The ability to listen quietly and stay focused on a patient is difficult but essential. Openly acknowledge that the patient may be right and you may be wrong. Offer to reexamine the facts. Chances are quite good that some of the facts associated with the case may have been overstated, either by you or the patient. After the patient has finished describing the problem, politely ask questions rather than pointing out all the places where the patient's statement of the facts was in error. By gently asking questions, the patient will most likely be able to see the errors on his or her own. This enables the patient to save face—and calm down.

Remember that the goal of a consumer-oriented approach requires you, as a health care provider, to put yourself in the patient's place. When in doubt, the rule of thumb becomes one of treating the patient as you would want to be treated, if you exchanged roles.

SOLVING PROBLEMS

Complaints are inevitable. If a complaint does not surface from time to time, perhaps the service being provided is not worth complaining about. Remember, however, that each problem or issue between two or more individuals can be viewed from several different perspectives. Be prepared to search for these divergent points of view, as you receive and review complaints from patients.

Do not go looking for problems, but be alert for warning signs that indicate areas of potential conflict. Obvious complaints—such as an error in the billing statement—will surface quickly and will not be difficult to identify. Many patients, however, indicate their dissatisfaction much more subtly, through statements such as "I have obtained information from another doctor that may be worth considering," or "Here are some facts about my history that I trust you will not lose sight of," or "The other doctor said. . . . " When a patient criticizes or challenges you, it is important that you remain calm and refrain from taking the criticism personally. Avoid allowing patients to transfer their anger onto you. Becoming angry yourself may cause you to overlook important information that can help resolve the situation more quickly and quietly.

Angry patients often need a lot of time to express fully what is bothering them. Try not to interrupt. Let them continue until they have finished. Then tell them you appreciate their point of view and acknowledge that you know how important this issue is to them. Probe all aspects of the case and assure them that all matters will be cleared up to their satisfaction. This technique will quickly remove the wind from their sails, and the angry patients will find themselves unable to continue their harassment. It is not important that the issue be totally resolved then and there. What is important is that patients feel they are being heard and listened to. Any disagreement, however, should be followed up with proper corrective action—and patients should always be notified of what has been done to resolve the problem.

Patients also often complain about the amount of time and attention they receive—or rather, *do not* receive—from medical professionals, particularly their physicians. Doctors should heed these complaints and change their behavior accordingly. The patient-doctor relationship may be the most crucial factor in determining patient satisfaction. Patients who feel that their physicians listen to their concerns and complaints tend to rate their health care service higher than those patients who feel they have little say in their own care.

TURNING COMPLAINTS INTO ROUTINE REQUESTS

Let the patient talk. Listen carefully, with an open mind. Ask polite and meaningful questions about background essential to this history and related problems. When patients become convinced that you are genuinely interested in their welfare, they will also become convinced that the care they are receiving is highly satisfactory.

To make a lasting impression, go beyond just letting patients talk; engage them in meaningful conversations about their health needs. You will soon learn how to judge the needs of each patient and thus when and how to end each conversation appropriately. Some people can talk and talk without saying too much, while others can provide a lot of information with only a few words. The ability to listen and subsequently to guide patients through these very important conversations will improve over time and with practice. Even if only a few minutes can be given to a patient, that time should be spent in a friendly, caring exchange of information, rather than in a brisk, one-sided rush of a visit that implies "I'm very busy and am only going to give you the facts about your health."

Possibly one in 100 patients will protest a correct bill. Perhaps the patient believes a second X ray or laboratory test was unnecessary. Or perhaps the patient did not fully understand the need for a certain procedure and, when billed for it, refused to pay. Most medical practices follow a standard procedure with an unpaid bill: They repeatedly send the bill to the patient over a period of months until, if the bill remains unpaid, it is turned over to a bonded collection agency or an attorney for legal action. This process can be avoided—and a great deal of time and expense saved—if an effort is made simply to discuss the unpaid bill with the patient.

When entering into such a discussion, treat the patient with respect. It should be assumed that the patient is sincere, honest, and responsible, and that he or she would like to arrange payment, or to find an acceptable alternative, for a debt justly incurred. Begin by explaining why the particular service was provided and that no attempt was made to overcharge, double bill, or conceal charges. Then listen attentively to the patient's response.

After exploring together all facets of the case, turn the focus to the specific charges listed in the bill. Give the patient a copy and explain each entry in detail. Acknowledge that, as the recipient of the services, the patient knows more about them than anyone else—and that he or she also knows what is honest and fair. By giving the patient a voice in deciding the appropriateness of the charges, he or she is likely to agree to a payment plan out of a sense of fair play. Patients treated in a personal yet businesslike fashion will, in all likelihood, also return to the practice for future medical services.

MAKING THE JOB EASIER
FOR THE HEALTH CARE PROVIDER

A surefire way to make your job, as a health care provider, easier is to find convenient methods of helping patients have their needs met. All aspects of the medical practice should be as streamlined as possible, while still providing comprehensive care. One place to start is with the avalanche of paperwork that often greets patients when they arrive in a medical facility. Avoid duplicating similar bits of information on different forms. A review of most medical records and registration forms reveals much duplicated information. In hospitals, this problem is often compounded by having the patient fill out similar forms in each department. By consolidating a patient's history and the forms with associated information into one concise set, the burden on the patient—and on the staff—would be greatly reduced.

When talking to patients, begin by discussing matters on which you agree. By emphasizing things that are mutually acceptable, you convey the idea that you are both interested in achieving the same outcome. As a result, you are more likely to have a positive conversation. If a difference of opinion arises later in the conversation, stress that the conflict is over the way things are being done, not over the purpose for doing them. Providers of health care need to take an adequate amount of time to explain why certain requirements exist and what has to happen to resolve the issues. When patients understand the need for doing something, whether it is filling out a form or taking a medication, most issues can be resolved to mutual satisfaction.

Make it your goal to alleviate the patient's immediate need, no matter how minor you believe it to be. If you treat a patient's problem on the basis of your perception of the importance of the issue, rather than on the patient's perception, you are headed for significant difficulties in communication. No one should have to prove their need for health care before receiving prompt and courteous service. Of ten typical patients seen in the doctor's office, at least eight will have average complaints, concerns, and expectations. All deserve the empathy of the medical staff. Patients should not need to justify why they have sought care. Instead, they should all be treated with an equal concern for their health needs and an understanding of their apprehension about the medical process.

Only through such appreciation and understanding of the reasons patients seek medical attention will it be possible to deliver consumer-oriented care. Although taking a few extra minutes to empathize with the patient will not significantly alter the provider's decisions on medical treatment, it will alter the patient's perception of that treatment. By approaching each individual who comes into their clinic first as a person and only then as a patient, physicians and other health care professionals will find that the same person will later leave the clinic a more satisfied, informed, and compliant patient, who will then return as the need arises.

HELPING THE REFERRED PATIENT

All aspects of case processing and associated details should be handled by a member of the receiving physician's staff, following the referral. This task should not be left to the patient nor to the referring physician. Forms to authorize the release of information should be signed by the patient, which permits the receiving physician's staff to acquire previous records and reports that may be helpful in understanding that patient's health problem and helps avoid duplication of tests. Forms with information on health history should be sent directly to the patient's home, along with a telephone number (preferably toll-free or collect), so that the patient can call if there are questions.

All forms and requests for information should be accompanied by a stamped, self-addressed envelope, to make them more convenient for a patient to return. Be sure to include a form that gives your agency the right to share any information obtained with other significant people such as other physicians, nurses, or school personnel. If a child is being seen by a doctor because of a learning problem, for example, it would be helpful if the child's school psychologist, teacher, or principal could receive a copy of the medical report. Vocational rehabilitative agencies or other regional, state, or federal groups may need a copy of a doctor's report for purposes of instituting financial, social, or training services on behalf of the patient. A patient may also be eligible for assistance to buy a motorized wheelchair through the Muscular Dystrophy Association or other agency. Before this can be determined, however, a copy of the medical report will need to be sent to that group. Once forms have been signed by the patient or his or her representative authorizing release of medical records, the staff providing health care can expedite the necessary follow-up services.

TIPS FOR PROVIDING GOOD SERVICE

- Remember that each patient you see today is there because he or she needs your help.
- Listen intently, pay attention to the patient, and be eager to help. The perception being imprinted in the consumer's mind sets the stage.
- Go out of your way to greet each patient in a friendly yet businesslike manner. Without being asked, identify who you are and what services you will be providing. Remember: The first impression you make will set in motion an attitude about total service the patient can expect to receive.
- Talk to the patient about his or her needs. Convince the patient that you will be working to assure his or her satisfaction.
- Assume the position that the patient is never wrong. Whether this axiom is true is not important; what is important is that you evoke a patient-oriented attitude when trying to resolve problems.
- Remember that the only way to come out ahead in an argument is to avoid the argument in the first place. Even if you are clearly right and the patient is clearly wrong, do not argue! You will not change the patient's opinion by doing so.
- Do not go looking for problems, but do learn to be a good listener. Probe for all factors related to the patient's problem; most can be solved by identifying the issues and engaging the proper services and resources to lead to resolution.
- Keep a friendly attitude when confronted by an angry patient; strive to find common ground that will help you both resolve the problem.
- If a disagreement arises, convince the patient that you are both after the same results. Make sure the disagreement focuses on methods, not purpose. Methods can be renegotiated; purpose should stay intact.
- Find ways of making it easier for you to provide good service to patients.
- Before being seen by the physician, each patient should be instructed to develop a list of questions he or she would like the physician to answer. This process will assure that patients receive answers to their main concerns. Be sure to follow up with a short letter to each patient outlining the results and what to do about them.
- Let patients talk about their problems and concerns and even vent their anger. Only then can you develop a complete picture of the problem and guide the patient ever so gently to a resolution.
- Do not hassle patients about their bills. Treat them as you would expect to be treated—with respect, patience, and understanding.

Chapter 6

Follow Up on Good Service

Many cases requiring the attention of health care providers are resolved at the time of the office visit. Others need long-term treatment. In both instances, it is important to make follow-up contact with the patient after the visit. Such contact will make it possible to monitor the status of that person's health. It will also promote a continuing linkage between that patient and the provider and will facilitate the consumer's satisfaction with the service.

Patient satisfaction is one aspect of health care that is frequently overlooked or taken for granted. A "halo effect" appears to be in place on providers of health care, particularly physicians: this involves a perception that the doctor can do no wrong, and that once care has been given, no questions need to be asked. Yet despite the extensive and excellent training and experience of physicians, they are human and, thus, fallible. Questions about the adequacy of health care services must therefore be asked of patients as well as of doctors, if improvement toward excellence in that care is to occur.

Medical services have generally been assumed by consumers to be of high quality, but this assumption has not been adequately tested. Only recently has the Joint Commission on Accreditation of Healthcare Organizations, for example, begun focusing its efforts on clinical outcomes and the development of parameters for a practice to judge appropriate quality.[1] Patient satisfaction is a very reliable indicator of successful medical practice. It needs to be continually assessed, if services perceived by patients as relevant and meaningful are to be offered.

EFFECTIVE FORMS OF FOLLOW-UP SERVICE

Effective follow-up services for patients can take a variety of forms. Patients should be asked to write out questions they wish the doctor to answer about their health problems. For their convenience, a place to list these questions should be included on the medical history forms that patients fill out upon their arrival at the facility. Personnel giving health care should still encourage patients to ask their questions orally, but putting questions in writing can provide added insight into the patient's expectations. In addition, the questions can serve as benchmarks to compare against, when a determination is being made about whether the patient's expectations were met.

If a patient is seen by more than one staff member during the process of evaluation, each person should review with the patient his or her findings from the evaluation. Every visit should also be followed up with a letter, telephone call, and/or report. Research has shown that such follow-up has a strong and positive influence on how patients feel about the care they received, yet it is all too often neglected.

Providing a letter summarizing and explaining the physician's findings and recommendations for care is one of the most meaningful services that can be offered a patient. It provides "closure" to the patient's questions. It indicates problems that were either ruled out or confirmed during the examination. The summary also provides a record of the current status and recommended direction of treatment. If the patient viewed the service received as satisfactory, he or she will likely continue to seek care from that provider. The summarizing report should be sent to the patient within ten working days after an appointment.

Follow-up may also include telephoning the patient to check on his or her medical progress. This technique is especially valuable after surgery or in cases where medications have been prescribed; it can help determine whether the treatment has had the desired results. Telephone follow-up also establishes a personal link between the doctor and the patient. If the initial treatment does not appear to be working, the physician can prescribe an alternative and/or request that the patient return for another appointment. Some practices ask the patient to call the doctor at specified intervals or whenever the need arises, but this approach to follow-up service has been found to have a low rate of compliance. At the very least, the organization should provide a toll-free or collect telephone number to make calls more convenient for the patient.

Return appointments also fall into the category of follow-up service. Many problems that require therapy or frequent checks on medication necessitate periodic appointments. Scheduling patients on a weekly, semiweekly, monthly, quarterly, semiannual, or annual basis sets up a systematic avenue of communication between doctor and patient. Such scheduling should always be done with the patient's needs in mind. When patients believe their needs are being met, they will remain undaunted in their trust and support of their health care provider.

Monitoring how well follow-up services are provided will prove to be a valuable asset to management when called on to reflect organizational commitment to consumer satisfaction. When an administrator is asked, "How satisfied are your patients with the services provided?" it will be possible to refer to current outcomes and speak of specific changes made to enhance services to patients. Only through systematic participation by patients in the evaluative process can health care professionals really know whether their patients are pleased with the services they have received. Evaluators of health care often recognize the need to include information from consumers in their assessments: whether, for example, the consumer felt a physician answered all questions or whether the consumer received a follow-up report. But those same evaluators often fail to include in their assessments the consumer's specific likes and dislikes about the medical care and service received. Many doctors neglect to assess objectively *any* aspect of their patients' satisfaction with services. Others collect information so sweeping that it cannot be used except in the most general way. Still others ask the wrong questions, leading to the collection of useless information.

> Cast aside what is thought to be the patient's need and instead ask the patient about his or her expectations. Once the expectations have been defined, it is up to the physician and supporting staff to fulfill them.[2]

Only by focusing on those activities that patients state are important to them can a consumer-oriented system be built on excellence that will meet the needs of both patients and providers.

INVOLVING PATIENTS AND THEIR FAMILIES
IN THE EVALUATIVE PROCESS

Patient participation in the evaluative process is valuable on at least two levels: (1) it improves care for individual patients, and (2) it makes it possible to compile data on the opinions of large groups of patients, thus showing ways of improving care for many patients. Through such compilations of data, researchers have learned that what patients often remember best about their medical care is whether they were given opportunities to ask questions of their physician, how their appointments were scheduled, and what kind of follow-up care they received. Research and experience have also shown that several other steps can be taken to enhance patients' experiences at the physician's office.

Patients should be properly prepared for a visit to a hospital or doctor's office. They should be reminded before their appointment about the kind of information they need to bring with them, including information about past health problems, current descriptions of symptoms, complete information on their health history, records of immunizations, information on insurance, reports of health care received from other providers, and so on. During check-in, each of these items should be reviewed with the patient. They should also be asked whether they have any special requests: Is there any doctor or insurance agency that should be sent a report of their visit? If the patient will need follow-up therapy, now is the time to authorize the forms for referral for such service. Make sure you obtain the patient's signature on the proper forms giving permission before releasing information on medical records to any other agency.

Just as it is important to prepare patients before a visit to the hospital or doctor's office, it is also important to provide follow-up service after the visit. This contact, although brief and typically inexpensive (by telephone or mail), affords an opportunity to monitor prospectively the results of the medical service previously provided. It also promotes a continuing linkage between the patient and the doctor and provides a way of examining patient satisfaction.

A good index of patient satisfaction involves comparing what kinds of services the patient expected to receive with what he or she felt was actually received. This requires thinking about services from the consumer's point of view. For example, what could a patient expect to hear when calling for an appointment? Would the patient's work schedule be considered? Could multiple appointments be scheduled for different services on the same day? This technique would not only save time and make the visit easier for the patient, but it would also reduce the risk of duplicating laboratory tests, X rays, and the like, thus lowering costs.

Patient participation must continue far beyond the hospital or the doctor's office. What happens to the patient after the appointment is all-important. Now the question becomes: Did the medical service resolve the patient's problems? If the answer is no, or worse yet, if a medical facility does not know the answer, the potential for a malpractice lawsuit exists, and for good reason.

The follow-up process may involve referring the patient to a specialist. Most patients are usually unaware of the services of specialists, so it is up to the examining physician, usually a primary care provider, to inform them of those services. In fact, many health plans require authorized referral by a primary care provider before they will pay for the services of the specialist. Matching a patient to the right specialist is an important part of providing service of high quality. Once the specialist has evaluated the referred patient, it is important that the results be sent back to the primary care physician. This assures a continuity of care that is in the patient's best interest.

GETTING CONSUMERS ACTIVELY INVOLVED

Health care providers often recognize the need to include information from consumers in an assessment of their services, yet they fail to conduct the systematic evaluations needed for such assessment. If an organization wants to provide patients with excellent care and services, then it must take the necessary steps to assess how well patient needs are being met. Active participation of consumers in this process is essential, and there are a variety of ways to encourage it. For example, consumers can be placed on advisory boards, committees, or task forces considering health care.

Such appointments make consumers full participants in the development of policies and procedures for the organization. Some health organizations have mandated that a certain number of appointments to or positions on a committee be reserved for members of the public. These organizations can clearly state that their services and methods have developed with full participation by consumers. Similarly, many federal, state, and private grant-giving agencies require the participation of consumers in governing bodies of all health care organizations applying to them for funds. The funding agencies believe such a requirement ensures that the public's opinions about health care and its delivery will be heard.

Unfortunately, what typically happens with this form of participation by consumers is that the organization appoints, elects, or recruits its own "friends." Such action defeats the purpose of seeking unbiased input from consumers to help assess patient satisfaction. Effective efforts toward consumer participation must go far beyond the token involvement of friendly appointments. If a health care organization truly wants to get an accurate estimate of how satisfied its consumers are, it must involve its patients—and not necessarily just its friendly ones—in the evaluative process.

Assuming the organization does provide care and services that are capable of meeting the patient's needs, the first step in the assessment process is rather routine: Just ask the patients what they thought of the services, either through questionnaires, follow-up phone calls, or focus groups. Some providers believe that this form of consumer participation actually places the patient in a position of judgment over the provider. It does, and rightly so. The patient should be the judge of how well his or her needs have been met, particularly since the patient is the one responsible for the final bill. Anything less than excellence is an opportunity for improvement.

Only with direct participation by patients does the evaluation of care and services become a valid process. It is patients' perception of excellence that determines whether their doctors gave them enough time to ask questions, or whether their appointments occurred at the times scheduled, or whether they noticed any health improvements after their visit. The people receiving medical services—the patients, not the providers—develop the most important perceptions that create answers to these questions. What a provider can and should do is measure the results of the patients' evaluations and then modify their services to improve any weaknesses identified during the process while continuing toward excellence.

HINTS FOR FOLLOW-UP SERVICE

- We often recognize the need to involve patients in the delivery of services for their health, yet fail to conduct evaluations to determine how successful our efforts are.
- Many forms of patient involvement are possible. Search for those most meaningful to the goals and objectives of your organization.
- Are the actual services being provided perceived as excellent by your patients? If not, why not?
- Patient involvement in the delivery of services will help you identify where improvements need to be made.
- Do consumers want to participate? Ask them; this is the only way to find out.
- Anticipate what your consumers expect from their visit to the doctor's office, and then make sure they get it.
- Patient satisfaction is that aspect of health care that is often taken for granted or overlooked. Make sure each patient receives answers to all questions, and actively involve them in an evaluation of the system responsible for delivery of their care. Send a short letter outlining the results of your conversation and what the consumer should do about them.
- Services to consumers go beyond their visit to your office. Follow-up communication, after the visit, is needed to ensure patient satisfaction.

CONSUMER SATISFACTION: A SUMMARY

1. Everyone needs and deserves excellent health care service. These services are more available now than ever before.
2. Health care providers must be more careful in considering patients' needs in the planning, delivery, and evaluation of their care and services.
3. Universal health insurance, or an equivalent result of current activity to reform health care, will make it possible for consumers to go just about anywhere to have their needs for health care met. Patients will eventually become very selective in seeking this service.
4. Consumers have a tendency not to complain openly to their providers about problems or poor service. They usually leave the doctor's office without informing anyone there of their concerns,

thus making it impossible for the physician to identify or correct the problem.

5. Patients should be asked for both negative and positive comments about the care and service they received. Negative information is extremely helpful because a problem (or just poor service) can be improved only after it has been identified. Positive comments support the ongoing allocation of financial resources so that the organization can maintain and perhaps enhance those elements of the service system noted as positive.

6. One way to provide good care and service is to think in terms of what the consumer wants. Patients are shopping around for health care more than ever before and are quite willing to forsake local doctors if they believe better service is available elsewhere.

7. Examine the system for delivery of care and services; focus on those needs deemed important by the patient.

8. Implement a consumer-oriented approach to health care. Train staff to become consumer oriented through a voluntary commitment to achieve excellence on behalf of each patient served.

9. Satisfied patients will inform others about the excellent care and service they received. This will increase the number of new referrals to the practice *and* increase the staff's morale, as employees receive more appreciation from patients—and higher salaries, due to the increased business that satisfied patients bring to the practice.

PART II:
THE MANAGEMENT
OF CONSUMER SATISFACTION
IN MEDICAL SERVICES

Chapter 7

Managing Outcomes

Survival in the contemporary practice of medicine will depend upon:

1. physicians' ability to adapt to less reimbursement for services provided;
2. consideration of the need to develop an increasingly large base of patients served;
3. the ability to remain or to become proactively customer oriented to attract and keep new patients; and
4. the development of strong linkages with sources who refer patients.

Thriving will require all the things necessary for survival and then some. To thrive, physicians will need to:

1. broaden their base of resources, both financial and programmatic;
2. reduce unnecessary expenses incurred by their practice;
3. avoid duplication of services and expenditures; and
4. improve operations and achieve excellence in the care and service provided to each consumer.[1,2,3]

Managers can provide an essential service by helping the medical staff orchestrate a contemporary practice. Such help will require minimizing the effect of adverse market conditions and maximizing the benefits of trends in reimbursement and capabilities for delivering care and services. Simultaneously, attention must be paid to shifts in a practice's market share while seeking out opportunities to provide new and/or expanded services.

When managers have used traditional methods to attempt a thorough assessment of innovations in consumer care and service and of the relationships among factors responsible for success or failure of the practice as a business that delivers medical services, these traditional methods of assessment have contributed marginal value. As resources continue to become even more scarce, managers must be able to conduct the business of medicine more proactively, with an eye on future requirements and probable changes in the market, while simultaneously taking advantage of current and past results associated with the practice. A solution to this complex problem does not exist in a vacuum, nor can it be identified by focusing independently on what are perceived to be the most important elements currently related to a successful medical practice. Instead, what is needed is a technology of evaluation for use by providers of medical services; such a technology must consider appropriately the simultaneous effects of all important indicators of success in the practice, enabling those providing the services to maximize their abilities to meet their current and future goals and missions.

In the practical sense (operations), the role of evaluation in the process of management is a matter of technique. An event occurs, and a record is made of its effects. Careful study of that record generates quantifiable statements that can serve as inferential indicators that can lead to explanations, interpretations, generalizations, predictions, and decisions. In the theoretical sense (reasoning), evaluation is a matter of using concepts, conceptual systems, constructs, models, and theories. An event can be most accurately studied if managers can delineate questions meaningful to the practice as a business, in measurable terms and of a kind comprehensive enough to explore all plausible aspects of each problem thoroughly. Such questions require the identification of key concepts or generative ideas that can lead and guide the techniques to be used. Thus, evaluation can be thought of as bringing together conceptual systems (at the theoretical level) and useful techniques (at the level of practical operations).

Many factors may account for the theoretical relationships underlying the practical acts of doing something. To ask or answer questions involving complex relationships and numerous factors, however, necessitates an approach that is suited to considering simultaneously occurring events and activities. If one focuses on a specific relationship, it is apparent that many of the factors theoretically relevant to the concerns of a manager are randomized, when only one or two elements are examined. We may seem to recognize complexities regarding factors that affect the delivery of medical services and operations, but we often fail to conduct analyses that adequately reflect the combined effects of the many elements responsible for the complexities.

Where change in the targeted populations to be provided medical services is rapid and continuous, managers must apply cutting-edge technology to maximize the efficient and effective provision of services. As one window of opportunity closes during turbulent times, others will be opening to those leaders in the provision of medical services who are ready to take advantage of the marketplace. The time has come to expand one's thinking about how to proactively address the amalgamation of defined needs and the provision of services. The proactive thought process opens one's mind to the use of multidimensional thinking and inferential technology, which can enhance the management of systems for the provision of medical services. Survival and, more importantly, thriving as a contemporary provider of medical care and services will require continuous attention to the factors that account for change in systems for health care delivery. It will also require determination of how, when, and to what degree the effects of those changes will hinder and/or enhance their provision of these services.

WHY MULTIVARIATE ANALYSIS?

A multidimensional or multivariate approach is well suited for use in the evaluation and management of systems for the delivery of medical care and services. Since a successful medical practice is based upon the appropriate mix of elements of service and needs for health care in the market to which services are provided, it is necessary to determine both the influence of market conditions on the provision of medical services and the influence upon each other of interactive services and needs.[4] Characteristics to be considered concurrently include, but need not be limited to, the following:

1. Operational elements of the practice and services provided:
   - Shifts in volume (number of patients seen)
   - Trends in types and timing of clinical activity
   - Systems for services providing information to management, medical records, functions of the business office, and communications with patients, to continuously improve quality of outcome
   - Ratings of consumer satisfaction and other factors
2. Changes in the market (three examples among many):
   - A competitor moves in across the street and your practice loses 10 percent of its patients seen for primary care
   - A business for which your practice has been providing services related to workers' compensation leaves the area and your income from operations decreases 7 percent
   - A health care purchasing alliance invites your group to bid on providing capitated health care to the employees of the companies the alliance represents (many of which reside in your area of patient catchment)
3. Financial indicators (three examples of many):
   - A new 2 percent state tax is assessed against your net revenues
   - Your practice is asked, by the HMO from which a majority of your patients come, to accept bigger discounts (from 20 percent to 30 percent of billed charges)
   - The resource-based relative value scale (RBRVS) and Medicare reimburse even less than was in the budget (budget reflected a 13 percent decrease while actual is 18 percent)
4. Longitudinal/historical trends and statistically significant changes associated with any important characteristic of your medical practice and/or the hospitals where the physicians admit patients.
5. Demographic shifts within the area of patient catchment that change the composition of the basic population of patients for your primary and referral practice

Multidimensional thinking provides leaders with an opportunity to consider the role of many factors in the success—or lack thereof—of the medical practice or of one or more medical services, and also the role of significant elements of the practice, for example:

- Income from operations
- Referrals
- Visits for ambulatory care and admissions to the hospital
- Overhead expenses
- Consumer satisfaction and other quantifiable factors

Both descriptive and inferential statistics are helpful in illustrating results and relationships that yield inferences leading to enhancement of the medical practice.[5]

Descriptive statistics are typically utilized in charts and graphs and include discussion about measures of central tendency (i.e., mean, mode, and median), and about variability (i.e., range, standard deviation, and variance). Inferential statistics yield quantities that are interpreted along the baseline of a distribution of statistical probability. The findings allow conclusions to be drawn from sampled data and generalized toward defined groups of the population. Inferential statistics are characterized by statistical significance, which illustrates (by a "level of probability") a significant departure from what might be expected by chance alone.

An individual uses descriptive statistics to talk about existing data. Inferential statistics refer to data that the individual does not have, for example "What do I need to know about today's practice that will enable me to plan for its future success?" Findings are generalizable (inferable) within "limits of probability" that permit the projection or prediction of results toward other, similar, populations. For example, a statistically significant finding at a probability level of 0.05 indicates that 95 times out of 100, the same result would occur again (without attribution to chance).

AN INFERENTIAL EVALUATIVE APPROACH

Like any other business, medicine is replete with information— to some degree, more information than is required to conduct business. A process is needed to enable medical managers to define, monitor, and influence changes in that information, to maximize the impact of the medical products and services they manage. That process is *inferentially based multivariate management*, used in conjunction with an established strategic plan (business plan). The plan, which represents a preset, agreed-upon direction for the organization, should be based on specific targets or goals in outcome (so you will know where the practice is meant to go) and on strategies with defined objectives, programs, and services that enable you to know how you plan to get there. The objective of inferential thinking is to take systematic advantage, by reasoning, of what is happening or has happened that is reflected in measurable evidence.

Staff members who are responsible for each aspect of the business need to develop related, quantifiable goals and objectives to facilitate the measurement of individual outcomes related to overall organizational efforts. Evaluations of performance, considerations of compensation (including incentives), and promotions should be based upon desired accomplishments of individuals and of the organization. Formation of the annual budget follows development of the strategic business plan, with rank-ordered consideration of financial support and the support of human resources for those programs, services, and activities identified in the strategic plan as priorities. Routine review of measurable (inferable) performance according to the plan is critical and necessitates at least quarterly assessment, with a comprehensive, in-depth analysis conducted annually.

A dynamic business/strategic plan is one that is receptive to changing conditions in the marketplace and is updated at least annually. It is a "rolling," dynamic, fluid plan that evolves proactively and moves in relationship to changing times. If the plan has embraced the organization's mission, it is likely to remain fairly stable, focusing on what your business expects to do in the long-term future. The mission would be supported by a vision statement outlining organizational hopes and dreams and how those who will benefit from the intended health care service will be affected. In order to write either a statement of mission or of vision, those in management need to agree on values at the core of their understanding of the organization. A statement of core values would reflect expectations concerning the business: how individuals should consider their role and their style of practice or management as it relates within the organization.

As threats to progress and opportunities for development are identified, inferential evaluation is needed to consider the incorporation of such effects, positive and negative. Attentive management with the necessary tools to address change is important to a dynamic plan. It helps minimize the effects of adversity while maximizing proactive contributions (not reactive). The desired outcome is consensus (agreement within the group) on those strategies, defined by reasoning in association with presenting market conditions, that reflect the commitments of the organization aimed at attaining its desired mission and vision.

Strategies may take various forms and shapes. They need specific definition in order to address issues concerning the medical practice as a business while emphasizing its reputation for service, its image, and its superior points of difference from the competition that need to be placed in the minds of its customers. Strategies provide direction for clinical and other revenue-producing supporting departments; they should be opportunistically oriented to take advantage of the marketplace. For example, "Here is a specific opportunity; here is how we will use it." Since it is not possible to fund all strategic initiatives sufficiently, each service or program should be rank ordered on the basis of its measured impact and importance in helping the business achieve success in its overall mission and plan. Financial and human resources should be allocated more richly to the top 20 percent of the rank-ordered programs that account for a majority of the success of the organization. Multivariate evaluation, specifically multiple linear regression analysis, is well suited to help rank order factors that are the most important predictors of defined success; this analysis helps determine what elements of service or what business activities account for a majority of the variance associated with indicators of business success.

Once the strategic initiatives and measurable objectives have been specified, inferential methodology can be used to facilitate planning and the alignment of resources with those plans. The method infers predictable outcomes within statistically significant parameters. Probability of a desired outcome is predicted by calculating the cumulative effects of important historical and financial factors and associated trends, with the desired business outcomes, through applied mathematics.

Model for Inferential Evaluation (MIE)

This model was initially designed and field tested by the author in 1969. Various applications over the years have demonstrated the utility of the inferential approach in major medical practices, including the Marshfield Clinic (Marshfield, Wisconsin), Gundersen Clinic (LaCrosse, Wisconsin) and, most recently, Ramsey Clinic (St. Paul, Minnesota).[6-11] The following general structure illustrates how the model operates:

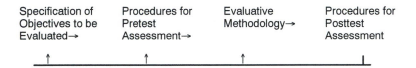

Specification of Objectives to be Evaluated→   Procedures for Pretest Assessment→   Evaluative Methodology→   Procedures for Posttest Assessment

Specification of Objectives to Be Evaluated

A most important step is the specification of objectives or targets your organization wants to achieve. The process requires a good deal of thought focusing on those elements that are indicators of business success. Often this is a multiphased process where it is necessary to understand surveys, studies, and/or financial and historical reviews in order to specify the objectives or targets of evaluation adequately. Since it is usually impractical and expensive to include in surveys and studies the entire population to be served, techniques for sampling the population and inferential statistics are used to provide results about the population in general. Such techniques are used routinely in political campaigns and election polls; they can accurately predict ultimate winners from rather small representative samples. If the study or survey identifies a need, managers must establish measurable objectives for exploring the opportunity to serve that need. It is at this point that relatively sophisticated inferential models are most helpful.

When the objectives to be evaluated are identified in quantifiable terms, they serve as benchmarks against which to compare future activity and results. To reduce the risk of a premature evaluation that might assess outcomes before the program has been given a chance to work, or to determine whether there are significant differences before implementing a new service or making changes in an existing program, it is necessary to collect baseline data in advance of introducing elements of change (interventive services or programs). Such information typically includes results of any sampling activity used to gather information about the population in general, and historical, financial, and operational data related to the activity or service under study.

Procedures for Pretest Assessment

Prior to instituting a new service or making changes in an existing program, it is important to know as much as possible about the conditions that may influence (or are influencing) success or failure. Steps taken during the pretesting phase include:

1. review of proposed strategies by managers;
2. review of results of existing programs or services, including findings from other institutions that may be appropriate for consideration in current business efforts; and
3. planning of specific procedures, time schedules, and monitoring necessary to implement the strategies.

When a number of strategies are under consideration, multivariate analysis can be applied to illustrate the relative benefits of each, within the limits of probability. This information, in conjunction with data collected during the specification of objectives, is used by managers to select the most effective set of predictors against which to measure the outcomes (achievements) of a program or service.

Information is collected and analyzed to demonstrate relationships among elements of the service or program and the objectives evaluated. The pretest findings are used to answer questions such as these:

1. How much of what should be accomplished by the new or changed service is already known or desired by the targeted population?
2. Does the population for which the new service or change is intended have the prerequisite behavioral or physical capacity, and/or do they need to benefit from the activity?

Answers to such questions will help managers structure an evaluation that can focus on the service delivered or the change in a program or system, and help them understand the effects of pre-intervention differences in need or readiness between individuals and groups served. The pretest assessment attempts to identify bias and other factors that can potentially influence posttest results. Once pretest influences have been identified, it is important to understand the potential problems they might cause and to eliminate those causes or control their impacts on outcomes. Most importantly, it is essential to identify and control each known biasing factor in advance of the introduction of a new service, program, or system (intervention), to promote a valid evaluative process. This step will help keep a focus on the interventions being considered, not the patients or groups of patients.

Managers require accurate information about the state of affairs surrounding the objectives to be evaluated, prior to implementing a new or modified service. Following attention to adequate safeguards and the implementation of proposed changes, it is then important to monitor data reflecting the new outcomes. This type of monitoring information is essential as a base for decisions on the maintenance, further modification, or discontinuation of an ongoing program or service.

Evaluative Method

Inferential procedures can help to reflect in statistics the complexities of systems for the provision of medical services that can benefit from data-based evaluation to provide reliable conclusions. A multifaceted question requires a multifaceted methodological approach to achieve an appropriate solution. Multivariate analysis was selected as the basic statistical method of this model of inferential evaluation. It enables managers to delineate, assess, and draw inferences from and conclusions about performance in the program or service from a multifaceted domain.

Multivariate analysis assumes that performance, behavior, or any desired outcome is subject to the influence of more than one variable or condition at a time and that adequate explanation involves more than a single variable or condition. If several variables are proposed as relevant to the outcome, it becomes necessary to measure both the influences of each variable on the targeted outcome or service, and their influence upon each other. Multivariate analysis allows administrators to reflect such complexities in the process of management, and adds the dimension of predicting future outcomes from past events. The power of prediction as a tool for management resides in the fact that such benchmarks enable rigorous testing of the adequacy of various trends in the business system—historical, financial, and operational—affecting the outcome of programs and the results of delivery of services, while predicting the necessary combination of elements accounting for the achievement of pre-determined targets (objectives) of the practice as a business.

Procedures for Posttest Assessment

Procedures for posttest assessment (assessment after the evaluative monitoring and predictions) are used to determine if, and to what extent, the specified objectives and targeted outcomes of the medical service have been reached. New business activity, and any service units with an increased allocation of financial and/or human resources, are assessed to determine whether there are any differences between relevant data collected from pretest assessments and posttest assessments. Posttest assessment measures progress toward achievement of defined objectives (the extent of difference within the limits of probability), direction and degree of inference, and predictability of results. Evidence is reviewed to determine whether the business is performing as expected, and what refinements are needed.

It is important to screen the information being collected, to detect defects in procedural design and in the process of implementing the service. The purpose of such exchange of information is to monitor the procedures for collecting data and to document the observable effects, not only at the end of the evaluative cycle but throughout the process, to identify potential problems and to correct the operation of systems for delivering the service, as needed. A dynamic, continuously self-improving business system is the desired outcome of multivariate management. The inferential evaluative approach embraces an outcome-based method for continuous enhancement of a medical practice, incorporating improvements (when they are called for) as a way of doing business.

In summary, the success of an effective business system will ultimately depend on:

1. devising quantitative, operationally defined objectives to be evaluated;
2. before the intervention (new approach) begins, establishing and measuring specific criteria associated with the desired outcomes;
3. after the intervention has occurred, comparing subsequent achievement with the predetermined expectations and standards of service; and
4. drawing conclusions from the new outcomes that enable the organization to improve, expand, realign resources (financial, human), *or* terminate features of the new service or program, in part or totally.

Chapter 8

Applications:
How to Implement, Interpret,
and Draw Conclusions

A series of examples follow that illustrates ways inferential management has been applied to the provision of medical care and services. The four stages of the Model for Inferential Evaluation have been considered in each example:

1. Objectives evaluated (or the intent of evaluation) have been specified in each case
2. The status of the environment or targeted population has been preassessed and defined by quantifiable targeted measures
3. An evaluative method has been selected to measure outcomes and reflect the effects that the service or program will have on standards of targeted services, financial results, and/or groups of patients
4. Quantifiable results (achievements) have been determined and illustrated as conclusions leading to recommendations for improvement, expansion, and/or other changes

This section presents examples that illustrate the usefulness of the inferential approach and demonstrate the ease with which it can be applied to any defined medical service and/or program. The various examples are drawn from different medical services and managerial settings.

EXAMPLES OF APPLICATIONS

Example 1

Marshfield Clinic, Marshfield, Wisconsin[1]
Number of Physicians: 400 (1993 MGMA Directory)
Number of Employees: 2,730 (1993 MGMA Directory)
Year Founded: 1916
Type of Group: Multispecialty

Objectives to Be Evaluated

Determine the level of consumer satisfaction among patients, parents, case coordinators, and sources who refer concerning medical and health care services provided. Also, determine what factors are most important to their current satisfaction and predicted future satisfaction.

Procedures for Pretest Assessment

Baseline measurement of consumer satisfaction was documented after the first six months of service, and thereafter at six-month intervals throughout the cycle studied.

Evaluative Method

Multivariate analysis (specifically, multiple linear regression) was used to predict the importance to consumers of various activities of medical service provided them. Analysis of variance (ANOVA) was the inferential method used to describe statistical changes over the course of the study.

Procedures for Posttest Assessment

Longitudinal assessment was used to determine the stability of consumer satisfaction across multiple elements of service. Five evaluative intervals were measured between July 1, 1975 and February 1, 1978, with the total number of cases (N) being 402. The most important factors related to overall satisfaction by parents (rank ordered) included: opportunity to ask questions, clarity of medical findings, ease of scheduling appointments, and progress made since medical intervention. Case coordinator results of most important factors related to overall satisfaction: how helpful medical findings were in determining specific educational activities for a child; and how well medical staff answered questions based upon a child's clinic visit.

Example 2

> Gundersen Clinic, LaCrosse, Wisconsin[2-4]
> Number of Physicians: 270 (1993 MGMA Directory)
> Number of Employees: 1,200 (1993 MGMA Directory)
> Year Founded: 1919
> Type of Group: Multispecialty

Objectives to Be Evaluated

Validate previous findings (Marshfield study) about consumer satisfaction among patients, parents, case coordinators, and sources who refer concerning the medical/health care services provided them.

Procedures for Pretest Assessment

Baseline measurements were provided by the results of the 1980 study.

Evaluative Method

Findings from the previous study were validated and expanded. Inferential analyses included multiple linear regression analysis, analysis of variance, and a matched pair analysis of responses to similar questions on both questionnaires/surveys (to patients and parents, and to case coordinators and sources who refer).

Procedures for Posttest Assessment

The longitudinal study in Example 1 (Marshfield) was extended from February 1, 1978 to July 31, 1979, adding 152 more cases (N = 554). Results from the first analysis (N = 402, from July 1,

1975 to February 1, 1978) were included with the results of the second analysis (N = 152, from February 1, 1978 to July 31, 1979). Statistically significant findings were noted and, as a result of the findings illustrated in the 1980 study, were attributed to changes made in the system for delivering services. Positive gains related to overall satisfaction were noted in all of the case coordinator questions with statistical significance (p = .05) present in eight of ten questions due to focused attention by clinic staff or helping the case coordinators interpret and apply medical information to the child's classroom. A member of clinic staff traveled to the child's school or day care program to complete conversion of medical data into the educational program. Parent results centered on two main factors accounting for overall satisfaction: how well medical findings focused on the child's educational needs; and having a clinic staff member travel to the child's school to implement medical findings into the child's classroom program in conjunction with teachers.

Example 3

Ramsey Clinic, St. Paul, Minnesota[5]
Number of Physicians: 231
Number of Employees: 473
Year Founded: 1966
Type of Group: Multispecialty

Objectives to Be Evaluated

Consolidate services given by a group of physicians (Ramsey Clinic) and the hospital receiving a majority of their admissions (St. Paul Ramsey Medical Center) to eliminate duplicated overhead expenses, improve operating efficiencies, and enhance revenues.

Procedures for Pretest Assessment

Audited financial data, data from the business office, and data on patient volumes prior to consolidation in 1987 were used as baselines, except for measures of outcome (against which to compare performance), which were made from the onset of consolidation

(1987). The main focus was on the period of intervention (planned change) measured from 1987 to 1992.

Evaluative Method

Basic statistical and inferential longitudinal trend analysis was applied to the data. This included multiple statistical comparisons to analyze the predictability of the results, and tests to determine statistically significant trends.

Procedures for Posttest Assessment

Longitudinal assessment was used to determine the effects of consolidation on the group of physicians over the six-year period. Combined clinic and hospital net revenue was a predetermined success factor. The top predictors of combined net revenue included: time (net revenue grew stronger as the clinic-hospital integration proceeded); referrals (new referrals rapidly increased and added significant fee-for-service revenue to both the physician group and the hospital); physician compensation (the physician turnover rate significantly decreased as compensation increased); and outpatient clinic visits (an increasing outpatient base led to more fee-for-service hospital admissions).

Example 4

Ramsey Clinic, St. Paul, Minnesota[6]
Number of Physicians: 231
Number of Employees: 473
Year Founded: 1966
Type of Group: Multispecialty

Objectives to Be Evaluated

Consolidate services given by a group of physicians and their hospital, to achieve a vertically integrated network of health services. Primary interest was in eliminating duplicated overhead expenses and streamlining essential combined operations in the vertically integrated system.

Procedures for Pretest Assessment

Audited financial data, data from the business offices, and data on patient volumes prior to consolidation in 1987 were used as baselines, except for measures of outcome (against which to compare performance), which were made from the onset of consolidation (1987). Data were taken from the physicians' group (Ramsey Clinic) and from the hospital (St. Paul Ramsey Medical Center). The main focus was on the effects of intervention (planned change) measured from 1987-1991.

Evaluative Method

Basic statistical and inferential longitudinal trend analysis was applied to the data. This included multiple statistical comparisons to analyze the predictability of the results, and tests to determine statistically significant trends.

Procedures for Posttest Assessment

Longitudinal assessment was used to determine the effects of consolidation on the group of physicians, the hospital, and the combined physician-hospital system, over the five-year period. Results for the five-year period identified three main areas that were responsible for combined clinic-hospital financial success: overhead expense reduction related to the elimination of duplication of business office systems; increased efficiencies related to improved production of clinical staff; and increased decision making due to integration of management systems.

Example 5

Ramsey Clinic, St. Paul, Minnesota[7]
Number of Physicians: 231
Number of Employees: 473
Year Founded: 1966 .
Type of Group: Multispecialty

Objectives to Be Evaluated

Physician-hospital organization (PHO) established in 1987 and last measured through 1992 was updated through reevaluation after adding data from 1993 in a continuously refining process of management.

Procedures for Pretest Assessment

Results from 1993 compared to those from 1992 that, together with trends of the previous six-year period, served as baseline.

Evaluative Method

Continuation of previously established longitudinal study. Methods for basic statistical and inferential longitudinal trend analysis were applied to the data.

Procedures for Posttest Assessment

Methodology for analysis of variance (ANOVA) was used to determine statistical significance of data from 1993 when compared with points of previous data that comprised the longitudinal trend for each defined target in outcome. Best financial outcomes for physician group in its history as a group practice were documented. The hospital also had very good financial performance. The best predictors of combined net revenue included (rank ordered): inpatient days (although average length of stay decreased as the number of patients increased); inpatient referrals (the number of referrals significantly increased ($p = .05$), leading to more hospital admissions of fee-for-service patients); outpatient clinic visits (number of outpatients increased, expanding overall patient base); physician compensation (compensation increased and physician turnover decreased due to joint clinic-hospital reduction in overhead).

Three additional examples follow, showing how inferential evaluation has been used to benefit management and/or to answer evaluative multidimensional questions.

Example 6

Public Schools, Mound, Illinois[8]
Number of Children Studied: 52
Type of Service: Special Education District
of Southern Illinois

Objectives to Be Evaluated

Determine whether a test of sensory-motor abilities (the Kinesio-Perceptual Test Battery) could predict racial identity among black and white students classified as disadvantaged.

Procedures for Pretest Assessment

Random selection of fifty-two disadvantaged children (twenty-six black, twenty-six white) without severe emotional or neuromuscular problems was made from the population of a rural public special education district in southern Illinois, to determine whether there were differences, and to what extent, in sensory-motor abilities.

Evaluative Method

Following completion of the Kinesio-Perceptual Test Battery by each participant in the study, basic descriptive and inferential statistical procedures were applied to the data. The means, standard deviations, and intercorrelations were obtained. Multiple linear regression analysis was used to predict racial identity.

Procedures for Posttest Assessment

Scores by black participants were compared to scores by white participants; findings reflected the predictability of race by the test battery in that black participants performed better ($p = .001$). The information could be further evaluated as an alternative diagnostic and training opportunity to improve the learning capabilities of black children. It should be noted, however, that the regression analysis was not cross-validated in this study; that would be required before results could be generalized to another population.

Example 7

> Bowen Children's Center, Harrisburg, Illinois;
> Mound, Illinois Schools[9]
> Number of Children Studied: 120
> Type of Service: Residence for Mentally
> Retarded Children; Public Schools

Objectives to Be Evaluated

Determine whether a test of sensory-motor abilities (the Kinesio-Perceptual Test Battery or KPT) could predict IQ among children in a residence for the mentally retarded.

Procedures for Pretest Assessment

To determine the usefulness of some commonly measured kinesio-perceptual abilities in predicting IQ, 120 children (sixty-seven boys, fifty-three girls) were randomly selected from a total population of 230 at a state residential center for the mentally retarded in southern Illinois.

Evaluative Method

Following completion of the Kinesio-Perceptual Test Battery by each participant in the study, basic descriptive and inferential statistical procedures were applied to the data. Statistical estimates of objectivity, Hoyt's analysis of variance, and test/retest reliability were calculated. Multiple linear regression analysis was used to predict IQ.

Procedures for Posttest Assessment

Scores by participants on selected items on the kinesio-perceptual test were related to their IQ. This correlation was found to be statistically significant ($p = .001$). Unlike other perceptual motor tests reflecting developmental growth patterns, the selected KPT items appear to be indicators of intelligence within this group of retarded children. This information could be used to supplement a diagnostic battery, providing a different type of measure that might offer a direct remedial opportunity to help the retarded to learn. The regression analysis, however, was not cross-validated, which would be necessary before findings could be generalized to another population.

Example 8

> Bowen Children's Center, Harrisburg, Illinois;
> Mound, Illinois Schools[10]
> Number of Children Studied: 120
> Type of Service: Residence for Mentally
> Retarded Children; Public Schools

Objectives to Be Evaluated

Determine whether a test of sensory-motor abilities (the Kinesio-Perceptual Test Battery) can reliably differentiate among those who need remediation and those who do not.

Procedures for Pretest Assessment

At a state residential center for the mentally retarded in southern Illinois, 120 randomly selected children were given the Kinesio-Perceptual Test Battery. A second random sample of 105 children from a public school was used to cross-validate the findings.

Evaluative Method

Descriptive and inferential statistical analyses were applied to the data. Measures of interobserver reliability and estimates of stability were obtained, in addition to predictive validity achieved by application of multiple linear regression analysis.

Procedures for Posttest Assessment

Cross-validation procedures were applied to the scores of both samples, from the state residential center and from the public school district. None of the cross-validated findings was determined to be significantly greater than zero. Such a result cautions against generalizing the findings beyond the parameters of the population on which the validity studies were conducted. Further application of the Kinesio-Perceptual Test battery is required before more meaningful interpretations can be made of the data.

Chapter 9

How to Design and Apply Surveys of Consumer Satisfaction

MEASURING AND MONITORING CONSUMER SATISFACTION

Standards for measuring and monitoring consumer satisfaction with medical care and services must be established in a manner acceptable to the patients, physicians, employees, administration, board, and community.[1] Reliable and valid techniques are readily available to assist this, but whatever technique is used, it is important that the survey be developed to reflect both the positive and the less than satisfactory aspects of the services evaluated. The first step is to reach an agreement among those who hold a stake in the service (leaders among the physicians and nonphysicians involved) concerning the criteria and methods that should define, measure, and monitor the satisfaction of health care consumers. The focus should remain on the patient's view of the care and services received. Any other consideration is secondary to what is important to the patient.

Recommended Approaches

Many approaches to construction of a survey are available. The following kinds of surveys have proven to be effective. Aspects of one or more of these examples should be considered for use in evaluating services provided by your practice. Costs will vary, depending on the extent to which each is implemented and analyzed.

Mail

Written surveys, mailed to patients after discharge or distributed to them at the time they are discharged, have proven to be one of the best ways to measure satisfaction. Well-designed questionnaires can be accurate and cost effective. Mailing them has proven to be more effective than distributing them at discharge or at the end of an office visit. If satisfaction with outcome is a major concern, then some time must elapse between treatment and this measurement. If, however, service provided during the visit is paramount, then it is best to measure as close to the visit as possible, preferably immediately following it. Some types of survey may produce results skewed toward those who are most satisfied, because indifferent or discontented patients are less likely to respond. For scientific validity, a survey must achieve a rate of response that includes at least 30 percent of the patients whose opinion was sought, but the national average is only 15 to 25 percent. To improve the response, a second survey can be mailed, or the patients can be telephoned for the information.

Telephone

Surveys may be developed to ask patients by telephone, either primarily or in addition to a mailed survey, about their satisfaction with the service provided them. Surveys by telephone achieve a higher rate of response with the information needed than do mailed surveys. The telephoning may be done by physicians, nonphysician staffers, or volunteers. Patients will realize the importance of these results to the medical practice, but it is well to provide training for those conducting the survey, to help prevent biased interviewing that may skew the results toward positive comments.

Videotape

Semiannual interviews may be conducted with a focus group, and these may be videotaped. The focus group promotes interaction among patients, families, and facilitators that can increase spontaneity and candor in the responses given. The facilitator of such a group can obtain immediate feedback on attitudes and opinions within the group and can thus ask additional questions that elicit more information on potentially problematic areas of concern. The information is available for review on the videotape. Confidentiality of testimony given by patients must be maintained. Outside facilitators may obtain more objective data, while insiders may be able to mend damaged relationships by following up on less than satisfactory services identified by the group (although videotaping an outside facilitator can provide that information). It will cost more to use an outside facilitator. Comparisons of cost should include the value of improved relationships with patients.

Professional Shoppers

Commonly used in retail business, professional shoppers can provide cost-effective feedback to medical practices as well. The shoppers actually experience services provided by your physicians. This method provides reliable results about the quality of service because it can make evident potential areas of dissatisfaction. It would be appropriate to have more than one patient experience various services throughout the year. Costs include such things as cost of care for participants, necessary meals, parking, and mileage.

Environmental Audits by Telephone

The old adage "let sleeping dogs lie" has no place in a consumer-oriented system. Use every method to uncover less than satisfactory services and, once these have been identified, correct the problems before they get big enough to see in other ways. There are probably an ample number of incipient problems with your practice that could be seen by someone looking for them. Reliable results on the quality of your services can be obtained by personnel reporting both the information they can obtain by telephone, and their firsthand experience with the community they phone.

SELECTING A SURVEY TO MEET YOUR NEEDS

The type of instrument used to measure, and the types of questions asked, depend totally on why the facility is interested in finding out about patient satisfaction. According to Stamps,[2] it is important to decide whether the facility desires specific information (e.g., the maximum waiting time patients will tolerate) or general information (e.g., whether patients are more satisfied with the provider's technical expertise or with the type of interpersonal communication experienced at the facility). Stamps categorized instruments to measure satisfaction as (1) super-informal, (2) slightly formal, and (3) fairly sophisticated. Stamps' review emphasized that even so-called "fairly sophisticated" methods do not have a well-developed technical ability to measure levels of patient satisfaction.

Super-Informal

Probably the most common type of solicitation of comments from patients, the super-informal method also generates the most superficial responses. Its broad, open-ended questions invite general responses. Characteristically, there are only a few questions, and those are usually direct, such as "How satisfied are you with your care here?" Typically questions are similar to the following, with some specific references:

1. What do you like best about the clinic? What do you like least about the clinic?
2. On a scale of one to ten, how satisfied are you with the care you received here?
3. Do you consider your doctor to be a personal friend, or is he pretty businesslike?
4. How did your visit go today? What were some of the things you did not like about your visit with the doctor?

These broad questions are simple to generate, easy to ask in a nonthreatening and informal way, and can obtain simple information that can be very valuable, especially if this is the first time patients have been asked about their perceptions of medical care. Answers generated by such questions, however, may include that what is liked best or least is "doctors" or "atmosphere," or that they "waited too long." Stamps notes that it is difficult to get negative responses from patients asked questions by the informal approach. When asked what they do not like about the clinic, they may respond "nothing" or "everything," leaving it up to the researcher to interpret. Asking one or two broad, open-ended questions immediately after a visit to the provider also may introduce bias, since responses invariably reflect what happened in that specific visit. To control for this bias, it is imperative to use a follow-up question to inquire whether the problem or benefit is usual or common.

Slightly Formal

Stamps describes the "slightly formal" category of measurements of patient satisfaction as characteristically longer, with a mixture of general and specific questions (most of them still open ended). This broad category can include many types of questionnaires and interviews of all kinds, short of the very structured approaches, but these surveys always emphasize the specific interests of the facility rather than more general questions about attitude. This type of questionnaire, for example, might be like one that was administered twice in five years to patients visiting a family practice clinic. The objective of that research was to determine levels of satisfaction specific to that model of care (family practice), and to discover whether patients were making use of this practice as the providers intended.

In this example, the social background of the patient population was predominantly lower class, and most patients were accustomed to receiving fragmented care from emergency rooms. Items on the questionnaire measured not only levels of satisfaction but also perceptions about health and illness (to examine patterns of use of the clinic), knowledge about the scope of services offered by the clinic, orientation to use of the clinic by families, and assessments of actual patterns of use. There were questions eliciting demographic information. In this (residency training) program, the professional staff made an intensive effort to educate patients about the scope of services offered and about the importance of family-oriented care. By the time the same questionnaire was administered for the second time (five years later), there were demonstrable differences in patterns of clinic use and levels of patients' knowledge, more positive attitudes toward the concept of family care, and higher levels of satisfaction. This is an example of use of a survey not only to gather information but also to change the behavior of the providers, with a resultant change in clinic use by patients and an increase in their level of satisfaction.

Fairly Sophisticated

Stamps sees questions asked of patients by fairly sophisticated surveys as more directed than in slightly formal surveys, and usually not permitting free responses. Figure 9.1 shows Stamps' example of a questionnaire asking specific items related to satisfaction and eliciting defined responses. This scale was administered as part of a larger interview of 175 randomly selected patients waiting to see providers in a private, fee-for-service group practice. A Likert-type response scale was used, values ranging from one (strongly agree) to five (strongly disagree). A high level of satisfaction was defined as a score of 2.00 (respondents had to agree with the statement classified to register as satisfied). In this example, the overall mean was 2.14, indicating moderate levels of satisfaction: 68 to 87 percent of patients responding either agreed or strongly agreed with each statement. On this scale, responses showed very little dissatisfaction with physicians and nurses, mild dissatisfaction with the support staff, reception area, and friendliness in delivery of medical care, and moderate dissatisfaction with prices, billing, and the system for making appointments by telephone.

OPTIONS FOR COLLECTING INFORMATION

The approach advocated by Kurtz and Boone describes three primary alternatives for collection of data: observation, survey, or controlled experiment.[3] No single method is best in all circumstances, and any one of these methods may prove to be the most efficient in a particular situation. Observational studies are conducted by actually viewing the actions of the person studied. Examples might be a traffic count at a potential location, or a check of license plates at a shopping center to determine the area from which shoppers are attracted. Some information cannot be obtained through mere observation of overt acts by consumers. The researcher must ask questions to obtain information on attitudes, motives, and opinions. The most widely used approach to collecting primary data such as this is the survey, of which there are three kinds: telephone, mail, and personal interviews.

Finally, the least-used method of collecting information on consumers is the controlled experiment. An experiment is a scientific investigation in which a researcher controls or manipulates factors affecting a group or groups to be tested, and compares the results with other results obtained from a control group for which those factors were not controlled or manipulated. Experiments can be conducted in the field or in a laboratory.

FIGURE 9.1. A Fairly Sophisticated Method for Measuring Levels of Patient Satisfaction

Questions	Strongly Agree		Agree		Uncertain		Disagree		Strongly Disagree	
	#	%	#	%	#	%	#	%	#	%
1. The physicians at _____ are very competent.	34	23.3	86	58.9	25	16.6	1	.07	0	0.0
2. The nursing staff at _____ are very competent.	39	26.5	80	54.5	27	18.4	1	.07	0	0.0
3. The _____ support staff (lab, reception, business office) are very competent.	25	17.1	79	52.1	31	21.2	7	4.8	14	9.6
4. The telephone system used to make appointments at _____ is efficient.	26	17.6	76	52.1	13	8.9	17	11.6	14	9.6
5. Medical care at _____ is delivered in a friendly and personal manner.	40	27.4	87	59.6	11	7.5	5	3.4	3	2.1
6. The reception area of _____ is very attractive.	42	28.6	80	54.5	14	9.5	7	4.8	4	2.7
7. The prices at _____ are fair.	19	12.8	85	57.0	30	20.1	11	7.4	4	2.7
8. The billing activities are efficiently handled.	16	10.8	85	57.4	28	18.9	14	9.5	5	3.4

Source: Stamps, P. Measuring patient satisfaction, *Medical Group Management Journal*, 31(1): 36-38, 40, 42, 44, January/February 1984. Reprinted with permission from the Medical Group Management Association, 104 Inverness Terrrace East, Englewood, Colorado 80112-5036; 303-799-1111, copyright 1984.

EXAMPLES OF SURVEYS

Although the collection of information on consumer satisfaction is not new, it has yet to be fully recognized as an essential survival technique in the health care profession. Other service industries have recognized the need, and have measured their consumers' satisfaction over the years, as in these examples:

Survey Found on a Table in a Restaurant

Figure 9.2 is a $4'' \times 5''$ card asking consumers to rate food and service. Notice the reference to a "promise" to personalize and highlight importance.

Survey Found in a Magazine

Figure 9.3 is a survey asking consumers to judge a product. Notice the statement that this company does not share consumer information with others. This statement offers protection for the consumer and increases willingness to evaluate the product.

Survey Received Following Automotive Services

This survey was received following services from an automobile dealer and service center (see Figure 9.4). Note the focus on improvement and the postage-paid, self-addressed return card.

Survey Found in Motel Room

Figure 9.5 is an example of a postage-paid, self-addressed postcard survey asking customers for general comments and/or suggestions for improvement.

Survey Done by a Department Store

Notice this survey's focus on simply checking responses and its request for open-ended improvement suggestions (see Figure 9.6).

FIGURE 9.2. Survey Rating Food and Service

Did we live up to our promise in:

	Excellent	Good	Fair	Poor
Food	□	□	□	□
Beverages	□	□	□	□
Desserts	□	□	□	□
Cleanliness	□	□	□	□

Time of Day _____ A.M. _____ P.M. Date _____

Remarks _____

How did you hear about us?

TV □ Radio □ Newspaper □ Friend □

Other _____

OPTIONAL

Name _____ Phone Number _____

Address _____

City _____ State _____ Zip _____

Please deposit in suggestion box at exit door.

Thanks very much.

"Where The Extras . . . Don't Cost Extra!"

Because you're important to us . . .

We Promise:

1. To provide a great variety of quality food, in unlimited quantity, at prices that represent a truly unusual value.
2. To provide a relaxing atmosphere in clean and pleasant surroundings.
3. To make your dining at _____ a truly enjoyable experience.

Did we keep our promise?

If you were not completely satisfied, for any reason, won't you be kind enough to tell us so that we can make it right. Of course, if you are happy with us, we'd like to know that, too. Please take a minute to fill out the reverse side of this card. We appreciate your business and strive hard to merit your continued visits.

"Where The Extras . . . Don't Cost Extra!"

FIGURE 9.3. Product Evaluation Survey

WE'D LIKE TO HEAR FROM YOU!

Send to: TREND enterprises, Inc., PO Box 64073, St. Paul, MN 55164

PLEASE TELL US ABOUT YOURSELF:

NOTE: TREND does not make its customer names and information available to any outside sources.

Name _____

Address _____

City/State/Zip _____

Phone ___(___)_____
Your age _____ **Sex** ☐ **M** ☐ **F**

Would you like to receive TREND catalogs? ☐ Yes ☐ No

Would you participate in future TREND surveys? ☐ Yes ☐ No

PLEASE TELL US ABOUT THE PRODUCT:

TREND Item # T-_____

Item name _____

_____

Date of purchase _____ / _____ / _____

Is this your first TREND product purchase? ☐ Yes ☐ No

Product was purchased by:
☐ Teacher ☐ Parent ☐ Relative
☐ Child ☐ Other _____

Product was purchased for use by ages: (circle all that apply)
1 2 3 4 5 6 7 8 9 10
11 12 13 14 Other _____

Place of purchase:
☐ School supply store   ☐ TREND Catalog
☐ Large Retailer   ☐ Other Catalog
☐ Convention   ☐ Other

Product will be used for:
☐ School   ☐ Home   ☐ Home school
☐ Church   ☐ Gift   ☐ Office
☐ Other_____

Is there anything wrong?
☐ Parts missing   ☐ Parts damaged
☐ Quality defect   ☐ Incorrect information
☐ Other_____

Please rate the quality of TREND products: (1 is lowest, 5 is highest)
1   2   3   4   5

We appreciate your comments!
Your ideas and observations help us create quality products that make learning fun. Please use the back of this form to share your thoughts with us.

Your comments are important to us!

_____

_____

_____

_____

_____

_____

_____

_____

_____

_____

_____

_____

_____

_____

_____

_____

_____

Thank you!

J	F	M	A	M	J	97	98
J	A	S	O	N	D	99	00

TREND
We make learning FUN!

Source: Trend Enterprises, Inc., St. Paul, MN, 1997. Reprinted with permission.

FIGURE 9.4. Automotive Survey

WE WANT TO BE SURE YOU ARE PLEASED

	yes	no
Were You Greeted Promptly?	☐	☐
Were You Treated Courteously?	☐	☐
Is The Work Satisfactory?	☐	☐
Was Your Job Finished When Promised?	☐	☐
Were The Seat And Steering Wheel Free From Grease?	☐	☐

Have You Any Comments? _____

_____

_____

_____

_____

_____

Name _____

Address _____

_____Phone_

**To Help Us Improve Our Service,
Please Fill In And Mail This Card**

FORM FWS-511 (4-81)   NORICK OKLAHOMA CITY

NO POSTAGE
NECESSARY
IF MAILED
IN THE
UNITED STATES

BUSINESS REPLY CARD

POSTAL PERMIT #54   LA CROSSE, WISCONSIN

POSTAGE WILL BE PAID BY ADDRESSEE

RAY HUTSON CHEVROLET, INC.

3232 Mormon Coulee Road   Box 1565

LA CROSSE, WISCONSIN 54601

Source: Ray Hutson Chevrolet, Inc. La Crosse, WI 54601, 1997. Reprinted with permission.

FIGURE 9.5. Open-Ended Food and Lodging Survey

Hoffman House

We have a 35 year tradition to uphold. Your comments and suggestions are truly appreciated.

Name (Please Print)   Date   Time

Address

City   State   Zip Code

Source: Hoffman House of Milwaukee, Milwaukee WI 53213, 1997. Reprinted with permission.

Survey Done by a Supermarket

Noteworthy characteristics of this survey include interest in comparison to other grocery stores and suggestions for improvements. Of special note is its interest in identification of employees who were particularly helpful and/or friendly (see Figure 9.7).

Survey Sent by a Member of Congress to His Constituency

Figure 9.8 is a trifolded letter-type questionnaire. Notice that it is not postage-paid (perhaps because of certain political sensitivities surrounding abuse of the "franking privilege" by politicians). Of special note is how the congressman is requesting the rank-order importance of issues from his constituents' point of view.

FIGURE 9.6. Department Store Survey

Store Location _____

Date / Time Shopped _____

Departments Shopped _____

PEOPLE...

	Yes	No
Courteous and Friendly?	☐	☐
Willing to help?	☐	☐
Knowledgeable?	☐	☐
Prompt and efficient?	☐	☐

Comments_____

_____

_____

_____

SERVICE...
How do you rate the following?

	Excellent	Very Good	Average	Poor
Return / Exchange	☐	☐	☐	☐
Gift Wrap	☐	☐	☐	☐
Other _____	☐	☐	☐	☐

Comments_____

_____

_____

_____

QUALITY...
How do you rate the following?

	Excellent	Very Good	Average	Poor
Merchandise Quality	☐	☐	☐	☐
Merchandise Presentation	☐	☐	☐	☐
Store Layout	☐	☐	☐	☐
Cleanliness of Store	☐	☐	☐	☐
Cleanliness of Restrooms	☐	☐	☐	☐
Cleanliness of Fitting Rooms	☐	☐	☐	☐

Comments_____

_____

_____

_____

HOW ARE WE DOING?
Please tell us about your shopping experience. What did you like? What can we do better?

_____

_____

_____

_____

_____

_____

_____

_____

_____

_____

_____

_____

_____

_____

_____

If you'd like to leave your name, address and phone number, please do so here:

Name_____

Address_____

_____

City_____ State_____ Zip_____

Thank you for taking the time to tell us how you feel. Your opinion matters to us!

Seal, and drop in the mail or at Herberger's on your next visit.

Source: G.R. Herbergers, Inc.—"Herbergers, the Friendliest Department Store in America," St. Cloud, MN, 1997. Reprinted with permission.

FIGURE 9.7. Supermarket Survey

Compared to other supermarkets, how would you grade Erickson's

☐ Overall service
☐ Courtesy counter service
☐ Deli service
☐ Meat department service
☐ Bakery counter service
☐ Produce department service
☐ Pharmacy department service
☐ Cheerfulness and courtesy of cashiers
☐ Overall speed and accuracy at the checkout
☐ Availability of employees to help locate hard-to-find items

So that we can reply to your comments, please complete the following:

Day Shopped _____
Time _____
Store Location _____
Your Name _____
Street _____
City _____
State _____ Zip _____
Telephone _____

Please tell us if an employee was unusually friendly or helpful and what was done to make you feel this way.

_____
_____
_____
_____
_____
_____
_____
_____
_____
_____

Do you have any suggestions on improving our store?

_____
_____
_____
_____
_____
_____

Source: Erickson's Diversified Corporation, Hudson, WI, 1997. Reprinted with permission.

FIGURE 9.8 Survey from U.S. Congressman to His Constituency

CONGRESSMAN STEVE GUNDERSON
NEEDS YOUR OPINIONS

During the 98th Congress we will face the challenge of critical issues such as reducing massive deficits, getting the economy moving, reducing unemployment and preserving our natural resources, just to name a few.

As we deal with these and other issues, I need your views and opinions to help guide me as I cast our district's vote in the House of Representatives.

Please take a few minutes to read and answer the questions on the reverse side. When you've recorded your answers on the return card, detach it, put a stamp on it, and drop it in the mail. We will tabulate all the responses and mail the results to you.

Thanks for taking the time to complete this questionnaire. Your responses will be very helpful.

Steve

FIGURE 9.8 *(continued)*

CONGRESSMAN STEVE GUNDERSON'S 1983 LEGISLATIVE QUESTIONNAIRE

PLEASE RECORD YOUR ANSWERS ON CARD AT RIGHT.

Answer yes or no to questions 1 through 7.

1. The federal budget deficit for fiscal 1984 could be over $200 billion. To reduce this deficit that would undermine economic recovery, would you:
   a. Eliminate this year's 10% cut in individual tax rates, effective July 1.
   b. Reduce defense spending.
   c. Reduce agriculture price supports.
   d. Reduce college loan programs.
   e. Reduce education funding.
   f. Freeze all federal spending.
   g. Reduce entitlement programs such as AFDC and Medicare.
   h. Reduce discretionary spending such as aid to education and local governments.

2. To reduce unemployment, the U.S. should:
   a. Establish federally financed, temporary public service jobs programs.
   b. Increase federal spending on public works (buildings, sewers, highways) that create jobs.
   c. Reduce the deficit and interest rates.
   d. Provide tax credits for hiring the unemployed.
   e. Increase funding for training the unemployed for jobs in other fields.

3. The Equal Rights Amendment has been reintroduced in Congress. Do you support amending the U.S. Constitution to provide equal rights for all?

4. Do you feel the economic policies of the Administration are beginning to work?

5. Do you think the Soviet Union is superior to the United States in defense capability?

6. Should Congress continue efforts to limit or prohibit abortions paid for with federal money?

7. Are you a dairy farmer?

*Choose **one** for each question, 8 through 11.*

8. To reduce surplus dairy production and taxpayer costs, would you favor: *(choose one)*
   a. A voluntary incentive program in which farmers are paid to reduce milk production.

   b. A cut in price supports.
   c. A quota/base system.
   d. Maintain present program of production assessment fees.
   e. Freeze price at $13.10 per hundred pounds.

9. As part of the tax package passed by Congress last year, financial institutions will withhold 10% on interest and dividend income beginning July 1; do you favor: *(choose one)*
   a. A straight repeal with the resulting increase in the federal deficit.
   b. A repeal and replacement of lost funds with other taxes.
   c. Retain withholding but provide exemptions for the elderly, the young, and those with small accounts.

10. Plans for the future development of the Mississippi River should include provisions for: *(choose one)*
    a. Commercial navigation.
    b. River rehabilitation and recreation.
    c. All of the above.

11. What action should Congress take on President Reagan's defense program? *(choose one)*
    a. Support a gradual growth in defense spending.
    b. Make reductions.
    c. Maintain present levels of defense spending.

12. Which **three** of the following issue areas concern you the most? *(choose three)*
    a. Interest rates.
    b. Inflation.
    c. Unemployment.
    d. Government spending.
    e. Welfare abuse.
    f. Agriculture.
    g. Government regulations.
    h. Education.
    i. Student grants and loans.
    j. National defense.
    k. Energy.
    l. Environment.
    m. Mississippi River.
    n. Dairy price supports.
    o. Elderly.
    p. Foreign policy.
    q. Women's issues.

13. Age: a. (18-24), b. (25-34), c. (35-54), d. (55-64), e. (65 and over).

REPLY CARD

(Please record your responses here, then detach
and mail this card. No envelope necessary.)

		VOTER 1				VOTER 2	
		YES	NO			YES	NO
1.	a.	☐	☐	1.	a.	☐	☐
	b.	☐	☐		b.	☐	☐
	c.	☐	☐		c.	☐	☐
	d.	☐	☐		d.	☐	☐
	e.	☐	☐		e.	☐	☐
	f.	☐	☐		f.	☐	☐
	g.	☐	☐		g.	☐	☐
	h.	☐	☐		h.	☐	☐
2.	a.	☐	☐	2.	a.	☐	☐
	b.	☐	☐		b.	☐	☐
	c.	☐	☐		c.	☐	☐
	d.	☐	☐		d.	☐	☐
	e.	☐	☐		e.	☐	☐
3.	.	☐	☐	3.		☐	☐
4.		☐	☐	4.		☐	☐
5.		☐	☐	5.		☐	☐
6.		☐	☐	6.		☐	☐
7.		☐	☐	7.		☐	☐

CHOOSE ONE

	VOTER 1		VOTER 2
8.	_____	8.	_____
9.	_____	9.	_____
10.	_____	10.	_____
11	_____	11	_____
12.	_____ _____ __	12.	_____ _____ __
13.	_____	13.	_____

Chapter 10

Measuring Performance Against Standards

If you can't measure it, you can't improve it.

Once you have focused your organization's objectives, goals, and missions, and chosen an instrument by which to evaluate its performance, you need to decide what data you will collect to tell you what changes to make in your organization, and how your organization is doing after those changes. Do the patients your organization serves perceive themselves as satisfied? The evaluation of consumer satisfaction with health services requires a fairly standard approach. First and foremost, focus must remain on a picture of satisfaction as determined by the patients. The beginning point, in development of a system geared to satisfying patients, is identification of medical services associated with the direct delivery of care to patients themselves. There may be other, different consumers of the same care, such as parents, teachers (if the patients are children referred by a teacher), family physicians who refer patients with special problems, or other professionals who coordinate care on behalf of a patient. A key element is the establishment of a database that reflects each consumer's opinion of how well the service is actually provided.

EXAMPLES OF STANDARD CRITERIA EVALUATED

- What information is supplied to patients?
- How friendly is the staff toward patients?
- How much concern for patients do patients perceive staff to have?
- How much nursing care do patients receive, and what is its quality?

- How prompt do patients find your service to be?
- What are patients' perceptions of your prices and billing procedures?
- How available is parking for your patients?

QUESTIONS THAT REFLECT FACT AND OPINION

Consumers must be asked questions that can elicit their opinions about the delivery of essential elements of the care and service received or about activities of prime importance to that particular person or group (the patient, referring doctor, school teacher, etc.). Careful selection of questions is important in developing assessments of patients' opinions of a particular service. The questions should be structured in enough detail to identify what they perceive as problems with the way care and service is being delivered. The following example presents questions used to assess satisfaction with services provided to children with exceptional needs in maintaining their health and learning.

Each question was designed by first identifying activities associated with the production of services for exceptional children at the doctor's office, and then selecting statements inquiring about those activities. An attempt was made to avoid duplication or similarity in questions. Staff members reviewed the questions for clarity and completeness, and then field tested each survey (the one for parents and the one for case coordinators) by asking people in each group to respond particularly as the questions applied to their most recent visit. Respondents were also asked whether the questions were understandable, concise, and important to them. Revisions were made according to the suggestions received. Focus groups of consumers made an additional review that led to final versions of the questions.

Questions to Be Answered by Parents

1. Were you given opportunities to ask questions?
2. Was there an explanation of the medical findings as they related to the education of your child?
3. Did you receive a clearly developed explanation of all findings after your visit to the doctor's office?

4. Were your appointments scheduled properly?
5. Has progress been made, since your child was seen?
6. Would a personal visit to your community by a member of our staff, to follow up on progress made by your child since visiting the doctor, be important to you?
7. Were you pleased with the overall service provided by our staff?

Additional Information

• Group membership. (During what interval of time was this child seen?)
• Is this your first visit to this doctor?
• Did you receive an appointment to return?
• Do you have any suggestions or general comments about the service and care received? (Provide ample space at the end of the survey for comments and suggestions.)

Questions for Case Coordinators

1. Were your questions on the medical evaluation of this child answered by our staff?
2. Was a distinction made between the medical and nonmedical needs of the child?
3. Were the medical findings helpful in determining specific educational programming activities for the child?
4. Did the medical findings clarify your understanding of the child's exceptional educational needs?
5. Were suggestions made by our staff about the child's educational activities appropriate to your local program and your community's resources?
6. Did you assist our staff in the development of a plan to be used when the child returned home?
7. Has progress been made since the child was seen at the doctor's office?
8. Did you receive from our staff all assistance necessary to deal with the child's exceptional educational needs?
9. Would a personal visit to your program's center by a member of our staff, following up on the child's progress since visiting the doctor, be important to you?

Additional Information

- Group membership. (During what interval of time was the child seen?)
- Is this the first child you have referred to the doctor?
- Did you have any difficulty scheduling appointments?
- How far do you live from the doctor's office (in miles)?
- Do you have any suggestions or general comments about service and care received?

SELECTING A FORMAT FOR YOUR SURVEY

Information on satisfaction can be obtained using a variety of methods: structured questionnaires, personal interviews, yes/no surveys, and many more. Select a procedure with which you are comfortable and one that obtains the information you are seeking. The format should permit longitudinal follow-up (i.e., it should be capable of monitoring satisfaction over the years) so that you can describe trends in consumer satisfaction that should correlate quite well with the success of your practice. Strengths and weaknesses in your service delivery system will be observable through this instrument. Weaknesses can be eliminated by focusing remedial attention on those elements of service that account for the perceptions of poor service. Strengths can be maintained (observed by continued favorable ratings and comments).

Standard administration of the questionnaire, collection of data, and procedures for analysis are recommended in monitoring service delivery. As problems develop that are reflected by poor ratings of a service, it will be necessary to identify the unsatisfactory elements by reviewing those tasks associated with the poor ratings. Once procedures or techniques have been altered to improve the service, it is important to know what changes in perception to expect. The new findings will need to be carefully documented and studied, to determine whether the proper adjustments have been made to lead to desired improvements in the patients' perceptions. Try to keep procedures and methods as standard as possible. This philosophy will maximize chances of systematically improving less than favorable services while maintaining those that are at acceptable levels.

QUANTIFYING OPINIONS: THE RATING METHOD

Most questions seeking information about satisfaction are answered either positively or negatively. A question such as, "Were you satisfied with the time the doctor spent with you?" can be answered by a basic "yes" (positive) or "no" (negative response). Perhaps, however, the patient was satisfied with the time spent but felt that more time was needed to receive adequate answers to his or her questions. If a strictly "yes or no" format for ratings is used, the patient would have to answer yes or no, but in this case either response would be less than completely accurate. One way to gain more information would be to add some space next to the question, indicating to patients that they can explain their answers there, if more is needed.

A way to obtain additional objective information would be to have consumers give ratings corresponding to their level of satisfaction on each question on a scale (continuum) of responses from "yes" (positive) to "no" (negative), 0 to 100 percent, a rating of 50 percent being average and 100 percent excellent.

Example:

"Were you given opportunities to ask questions?"

No (negative). . . . . Yes (positive)

0% 10% 20% 30% 40% 50% 60% 70% 80% 90% 100%

Average

The scaled format for ratings provides respondents an opportunity to describe their perceptions of how satisfactorily a particular service was delivered. Using the question in the example as a point of reference, let's say that "yes," the parents were given the opportunity to ask questions, but the opportunity was poor. Perhaps they were rushed, not listened to, or cut off before they could fully comprehend the answer given by their doctor. To be honest, the parents would have to answer "yes"; they were given opportunities to ask questions. They could, however, circle a "poor yes" response (below 50 percent), on the rating scale. This should be viewed as unsatisfactory. A follow-up, checking on statements found in the section reserved for comments and suggestions at the end of the questionnaire, could very well reveal the reasons for poor ratings. Another way to obtain an explanation of poor ratings would be to telephone or write the respondent and ask them about it while explaining how the information will be used to improve operations for the patient's next visit.

PROCEDURES FOR ADMINISTERING SURVEYS

How and when one assesses consumer satisfaction will, in large part, depend upon the type of patient being served and under what conditions. Different procedures are recommended for different types of patients. For example, the terminally ill patient has a different set of requirements for satisfaction than does a high-risk infant provided service through a perinatal center. Likewise, a patient being seen for problems with a cleft lip will have different requirements than will a postcardiac patient seen at the pacemaker clinic. Once specific important questions have been determined, it is possible to plan the strategy for administering the survey. How long should one wait to measure satisfaction? Will the consumer be better able to recall the service if asked about it close to the time it occurred? The honest answer is "yes—and no." Yes, the patient will remember more explicitly how long was the wait to see the doctor, whether the receptionist was snippy or nice, and whether his or her conversation with the insurance clerk was appropriate. It may, however, take more time to determine whether medical intervention has positively influenced the life of, for example, a child with a learning disability, a behavioral problem, or poor development of speech and language, or, for example, the child receiving physiotherapy for cerebral palsy.

Children with special problems in maintaining health and learning provided the example below. In this case, there is a need to make follow-up contact after the visit to the doctor's office, to see whether the medical intervention helped the child. For purposes of this example, a six-month interval after the visit was initially set as the time for that follow-up (the interval was subsequently changed to four months, as that appeared to be more appropriate to meeting the needs of the program). The questionnaires used in the survey were sent to both the child's parents and his case coordinator, six months after the child's visit to the clinic. (Initially, an annual questionnaire had been sent, but there were complaints from consumers that they were not able, a year after it occurred, to remember enough details about the nature and effectiveness of the service received.) The questionnaire was accompanied by an introductory letter that explained the reason for sending the questionnaire and the process by which they should rate their satisfaction.

Example 1: Letter for Parents

Study Number_____
RE:____(Child's Name)____
Medical Chart #_____

Dear Parents:

The members of the staff of the doctor's office are interested in knowing how you feel about the treatment you and your child received when seen here. Listed on the following pages are questions concerning various parts of the services provided. Please rate each of the questions to correspond to your level of satisfaction particularly concerning your most recent visit. Circle the percentage (%) of your satisfaction relative to each item questioned. A rating of 50 percent is average and 100 percent is excellent. A rating above 50 percent indicates a positive (favorable) response concerning the item in question; a rating of less than 50 percent indicates a negative (less than favorable) response.

For example:

"The amount of time staff spent with your child was satisfactory?"

NO (Negative)   YES (Positive)

0%   10%   20%   30%   40%   50%   60%   70%   80%   90%   100%

Please complete and return the questionnaire in the enclosed stamped envelope within the next five days. To those whose questionnaires have not been returned after five days, members of our staff will make follow-up contact to help them to complete it. If you have any questions, please contact me, toll free, at 1-800-000-0000, and I will answer them for you. Thank you for taking the time to respond to this questionnaire. Your response will help improve our service to you.

Sincerely,
(Insert name of key person to contact with questions)
Service Management

Example 2: Letter for Case Coordinators

Study Number_____
RE:____(Child's Name)____
Medical Chart #_____

Dear Coordinator:

The members of the staff of the doctor's office are interested in knowing how you feel about the treatment received by the above-named child whom you referred to us. Listed on the following pages are questions concerning various parts of the services provided. Please rate each of the questions to correspond to your level of satisfaction particularly concerning the most recent visit. Circle the percentage (%) of your satisfaction relative to each item. A rating of 50 percent is average and 100 percent is excellent. A rating above 50 percent indicates a positive (favorable) response concerning the item in question; a rating of less than 50 percent indicates a negative (less than favorable) response.

For example:

"Was an orderly schedule of appointments made for the referred child?"

NO (Negative)   YES (Positive)

0%   10%   20%   30%   40%   50%   60%   70%   80%   90%   100%

Please complete and return the questionnaire in the enclosed stamped envelope within the next five days. To those whose questionnaires have not been returned after five days, members of our staff will make follow-up contact to help them to complete it. If you have any questions, please contact me, toll free, at 1-800-000-0000, and I will answer them for you. Thank you for taking the time to respond to this questionnaire. Your response will help improve our service to you.

Sincerely,
(Insert name of key person to contact with questions)
Service Management

The parents and case coordinator for each child were each mailed a questionnaire, complete with a self-addressed, stamped envelope for its return. If the initial questionnaire was not returned, a second survey was sent, and if that was not returned it was followed by a telephone call to secure the information.

Example of Second Letter

Re: A follow-up note to remind you to return the questionnaire sent to you on (specify date) for: (child's name)

Dear_____:

This letter is being sent to you as a reminder to return the questionnaire originally sent to you on (specify date). We are very interested in your evaluation of our services and will modify the program to best meet your needs.

Attached is a duplicate copy of the original questionnaire sent to you, along with a stamped, self-addressed envelope for returning it by mail. Please return the completed questionnaire immediately. If you have questions, please contact me toll free at 1-800-000-0000, and I will answer them for you. Thank you!

Sincerely,
(Insert name of key person to contact with questions)
Service Management

This method of follow-up serves two useful purposes: (1) It promotes a continuing linkage between patient and doctor by giving staff members a reason to talk to those who consume their services, about a subject of primary interest to both of them—the health and progress of the patient and family; (2) If it happened that the services provided were less than favorable, staff members have a chance to salvage some good by asking what could be done to correct the problems. This method proves to be extremely valuable in securing information about satisfaction in difficult cases. Once the problems are identified, those that can be resolved are resolved. Although some problems are not resolved to everyone's satisfaction, staff members do learn from their mistakes to avoid similar events during future encounters with patients.

COLLECTION OF INFORMATION

The collection of information about satisfaction must be a logical outgrowth or product of the process by which it is obtained. It is most helpful to look at the information from two perspectives: (1) that of the individual patient's case, and (2) that of the individual case compared to results in the group overall. The process allows one to monitor the effects of prescribed services on each patient, and collectively on groups of similar patients receiving the same services. Since the primary aim is to monitor the delivery of services over specified periods of time, such as a calendar year or fiscal year, or biannually or quarterly, it is not necessary to follow the same patient indefinitely. Instead, profiles are obtained concerning how satisfactorily certain activities are being rated, by asking many patients with similar needs to participate. If activities remain fairly standard from one evaluative interval to the next, the collective rating of average satisfaction in the group for each element can be used as an indicator of satisfactory or unsatisfactory service across the population receiving the service (Figure 10.1).

Individual ratings are easily interpreted, since you can pull each person's medical chart and compare the official record to his or her specific levels of satisfaction. Using the questionnaire on satisfaction as a base of information, one can tell (among other things) (1) whether the patient is satisfied with each important activity of

FIGURE 10.1. Summarized Follow Up

Study Number _____ Medical Chart # _____

Name of Patient _____ Parent _____

Date Form Returned _____ Case Coordinator _____

Date Seen By Doctor _____ Diagnosis _____

Referral Source (Check One): Self (or parent) _____

Physician _____ Social Worker _____

Nurse _____ Teacher _____

Psychologist _____ Other (specify) _____

Data on questionnaires from parents (% response to each question, data from filled in blanks)

Ratings of Satisfaction

Question #1 _____

Question #2 _____

Question #3 _____

Question #4 _____

Question #5 _____

Question #6 _____

Question #7 _____

Comments and suggestions: _____

_____

_____

Department(s) seen by: _____ dates: _____

First visit to doctor? ___yes ___no

Received return appointment? ___yes ___no

    If yes, list dates and departments for return visits

Distance patient traveled to doctor's office

(check one): ___ up to 20 miles ___20-100 miles ___over 100 miles

Data on questionnaires from case coordinators (% response to each question, data from filled-in blanks)

Ratings of Satisfaction

Question #1 _____

Question #2 _____

Question #3 _____

Question #4 _____

Question #5 _____

Question #6 _____

Question #7 _____

Question #8 _____

FIGURE 10.1 *(continued)*

Question #9_____

Question #10_____

Department(s) seen by:_____ dates:_____

First child you've referred to the center? _____ yes_____ no

Did you receive a medical report within ten days following the child's visit?

Did you have any difficulties scheduling appointments?

How far do you live from the center (in miles)?

Title of case coordinator (physician, public school nurse, teacher)
Comments and suggestions:_____

your service, (2) what particular complaints they have, (3) how long it took them to receive reports, and (4) how they rated your overall service. If the consumer is having difficulty with the insurance department in processing a claim, or difficulty with getting a report from a certain doctor, his or her concerns would likely be explained in the section eliciting comments, at the end of the questionnaire. Problems associated with individual cases are corrected as they are identified by a review of each questionnaire.

Variations can be built into the format used for recordkeeping, to account for changes, special effects, or any other elements. The format should remain simple and clear, to ensure that the person responsible for processing data has accurately defined the information in preparation for processing.

HINTS TO IMPROVE SERVICE

- Patient satisfaction means that the needs of patients in receiving care are met—the consumers' opinions are the determinant of satisfaction and excellence is the goal.
- Select questions for consumers that seek their critical examination of the care and services being provided—the questions chosen should relate to the most important parts.
- Once selected, the methods used to obtain information on consumer satisfaction should remain as standard as possible, to avoid misinterpretation.

Chapter 11

Collection and Management of Data

Systematic procedures are required to manage information about consumers effectively.[1,2,3] The tasks to be considered in this process begin with the clerical duties associated with coordination of patients to be surveyed and lead up to and include the manual or computerized preparation of data for evaluation. The evaluative system can be managed day-to-day at a clerical level to avoid excessive costs associated with frequent involvement by physicians, who would give up time seeing patients, or by executive administrative personnel.

If the number of consumers surveyed is relatively small and the data requirements are few, the data can be prepared manually. A computerized system is recommended, which becomes a necessity when a large number of patients are to be included and/or sophisticated procedures for using the data are desired (e.g., complex methods for tracking patients, statistical analysis, mathematical comparisons of data from one time period to the next, and the like). Since the system is adaptable to a one-person office or to a large medical group health plan or hospital, procedures discussed in this section apply to both manual and computerized operations.

CENTRAL COORDINATION

A central coordinator is needed to oversee operations. The required duties should be assigned to a person with good organizational, clerical, and interpersonal communication skills to monitor the evaluation process. A variety of general duties are associated with the role of coordinator. A primary responsibility is to identify obvious problems with the system and to screen each questionnaire for complaints by patients.

The coordinator must be knowledgeable about the specific health practice under evaluation and be able to answer questions that arise. Although the coordinator does not have to be a provider of health care services, it is important for this person to spend time regularly with the team to observe and discuss the nature and extent of services provided. It is important for the coordinator to be viewed as a team member rather than as a "police officer" type snooping into the business of other staff. The interaction between coordinator and medical staff should be as a partnership, with clear, open lines of communication.

Activities of Central Coordination

Communication

The coordinator must communicate with medical staff to determine which patients (and/or their representatives) are to be surveyed, on what schedule. Methods for selecting from patient populations may vary considerably from truly randomized to stratified sampling procedures since they may use a quota system to include only patients with strict diagnostic or demographic characteristics. As an example: in the care of arthritis, there may be a need specifically to evaluate services provided to children with juvenile rheumatoid arthritis (JRA), since the criteria for diagnosis and treatment vary considerably depending upon whether the physician is a rheumatologist or pediatrician. By evaluating services provided to patients with JRA, it is possible to compare aspects of consumer satisfaction to the types of physicians who provided service.

The schedule for sending out questionnaires will depend upon specific needs of consumer and provider. An interval should be used that allows ample time between medical intervention (satisfaction with service provided by professionals) and evaluation (completing questionnaire) so that some objective judgments can be made by the consumer about the benefit and quality of service received. For example, patients seen in a genetics and birth defects clinic may have to wait for two months or more for the results of special chromosomal studies sent to regional laboratories for analysis. Although these patients can rate and comment on some activities associated with this special program of service, a composite report of findings may not be possible for months. In this case, a four- to six-month evaluative interval could be established after a visit to the genetics and birth defects specialist before mailing questionnaires, to include results of chromosomal analysis in the evaluation, or multiple surveys could be sent asking questions at different points in time. This example can be contrasted with a survey of patients from a pacemaker clinic, where questionnaires are mailed out thirty days following care. Staff running a pacemaker service may believe that thirty days is enough time for their patients to render judgments about the benefit and quality of services provided.

Mailing Lists

Develop a mailing list and send questionnaires (complete with a letter to the consumers explaining the purpose of evaluation); always attach a stamped, self-addressed envelope for returning the questionnaire. Each patient included in the evaluative program should be identified for purposes of follow-up (with an identifier not duplicated in the study) that should appear on the coordinator's mailing list and on the questionnaire itself. The same identifier (e.g., a number) would go on all future correspondence for purposes of tracking the patient. A limit should be set on time for completion of the questionnaire, asking that it be returned, for example, within five days. A stamped, self-addressed envelope for return mail is mandatory to assure the best possible response. The coordinator's name should appear on the return envelope to ensure proper processing when it is mailed back. It is important to include a clearly written letter introducing the consumer to the evaluative process. Instructions should define the procedure for scoring and the person to contact (by name and telephone number) if questions should arise during completion of the survey.

Here is an example of an introductory letter:

Patient #
Maternal High-Risk Clinic
Code for Specialty Service
Number for Tracking
Today's Date

Dear Patient (use first name):

We are interested in knowing how you feel about the treatment you received when last seen at the health center for special services. Listed on the following pages are questions relating to various parts of your experiences at the Maternal High-Risk Clinic.

Please rate each of the questions corresponding to your level of satisfaction. A rating of 50 percent is average and 100 percent is excellent. A rating above 50 percent indicates a positive (satisfied) response and a rating below 50 percent indicates a negative (unsatisfied) response. Circle the percentage (%) of satisfaction you have for each question.

Example Question: "Was the amount of time staff at the clinic spent with you satisfactory?"

NO   (Negative)   YES   (Positive)
(Not Satisfied)   (Satisfied)

0% 10% 20% 30% 40% 50% 60% 70% 80% 90% 100%

Complete and return the questionnaire in the enclosed, stamped envelope within the next five days. For those questionnaires not returned, staff at the clinic will contact you to help with its completion.

Thank you for taking the time to respond to this questionnaire. Your response will help improve our service to you.

Sincerely,

Employee Name
Patient Services Coordinator
Telephone 1-800-000-0000

A second questionnaire accompanied by a personalized reminder, a letter requesting completion of the survey, should be sent out to those who do not respond to the first mailing. (Waiting two weeks before sending the follow-up questionnaire should allow adequate time.) If there is no response to the second questionnaire, a contact should be made by telephone to obtain the consumer's opinions (two weeks following mailing of second questionnaire would be long enough to wait before calling).

Here is an example of a personalized reminder accompanying a follow-up mailing:

Today's Date
Re: Questionnaire sent to you on March 20, 1998, by the Coordinator of the Maternal High-Risk Clinic
Clinic Chart #

Dear _____ :

This letter is to remind you to return the questionnaire originally sent to you on March 20, 1998. We are very interested in your evaluation of our services and will modify the program at the Maternal High-Risk Clinic to best meet your needs.

Attached is a duplicate copy of the original questionnaire along with a stamped, self-addressed envelope for returning it by mail. Please return completed questionnaire immediately. Thank you!

Sincerely,

Employee Name
Patient Coordinator
Telephone: 1-800-000-0000
Enclosures

Screening for Problems

Screen each returned questionnaire and resolve identifiable problems. A primary task of the coordinator is to review thoroughly each questionnaire returned. The coordinator should look for poor ratings below 50 percent and for extreme variations from one patient to the next in their ratings or comments on the same person or service. Negative "free response" comments may appear at any point in the survey and often correlate highly with ratings of poor and extremely poor satisfaction. A particular staff member may be singled out as providing superior or inferior service. In either case, those who are mentioned should be informed of it. One way of doing this is to make a copy of the questionnaire and send it to them along with a note explaining the situation. If the information is good, it will reinforce continued good care. If the news is bad, it should serve to encourage improved performance on those activities noted in the questionnaire that pertain to the situation.

Minor problems will be expressed that can be resolved immediately. These typically include oversights: neglecting to send copies of medical reports to appropriate individuals/agencies, to develop/send orders for special therapy to service providers in the patient's home community, to bill services to insurance rather than directly to patients, to renew expired prescriptions for drugs, to set up return appointments appropriately, and the like. The list could go on, but in essence these problems are quickly resolvable and should be handled by the coordinator when they are identified on the survey.

Flagrant or serious grievances that reflect on the nature of medical care provided or some other significantly discrediting aspect of the health service should be addressed differently. Most health care providers have established policies to follow when complaints occur. These rules should be followed when a grievance is found in a questionnaire. Each group or agency in health services has (or should have) a procedure whereby the medical director, chief health officer, professional practice committee, or senior administrator is requested to review the complaint. If the grievance is validated as confirmed by review of the record, witnesses, or other methods (or a combination thereof), the staff member involved should be approached on the matter by the proper officials. The problem may be resolved by an initial confrontation at this level, or it may need to go to other decision makers depending upon organizational policy. The coordinator's role at this point is one of collecting data and presenting the facts (gathered from the questionnaire, medical record, and other available testimony) to the proper official in charge. Following this procedure, the coordinator monitors the delivery of future service to determine the presence of similar problems and reports back to the proper governing body as needed.

After each questionnaire is screened and identifiable problems are resolved, the coordinator sees that the survey is prepared for data processing. Clarity is important in:

- expressing how data are to be prepared;
- editing data prepared for processing, before analysis (e.g., checking on scoring codes used to translate data for analysis, making sure complete information on each patient is included, and verifying that the scores recorded for data analysis match those on the questionnaires); and
- verifying and confirming results for interpretation.

It is customary for the coordinator to keep the original copy of each questionnaire on file, after data have been obtained for processing as a long-term care management benchmark. This procedure provides the opportunity to review questions that may come up in the future for a patient who has been previously treated. Also, as a patient becomes involved in the evaluative study over a period of years, a profile of that consumer's individual satisfaction will be on record. This information is applicable for longitudinal review.[4,5] The record of satisfaction will reflect the consumer's opinion of medical services, its direction (positive or negative), and its magnitude (percentage) of response. Once the specific level of service expected by the consumer has been defined in relation to services available, it becomes a routine task to monitor how satisfied he or she is with what is received. Less-than-favorably viewed services are identified by this process, which is the first step in eliminating deficiencies and improving satisfaction with care and services toward excellence.

REQUIREMENTS FOR COMPUTERIZED PROCESSING

Prepare Questionnaires for Data Processing and Analysis

Each survey must be reviewed to see that it has been properly completed and is ready to be entered (i.e., translated for computing purposes through scanning or data entry) or to be manually recorded on summarizing sheets for processing. Again, if the patient population to be surveyed is large or the needs for information from the data are sophisticated (e.g., complex patient-tracking methods, statistical analysis, mathematical comparisons of data from one evaluative interval to the next) or both, it is recommended that computer-assisted services be used.

Format for the Questionnaire

The manner in which questions are presented to the patient is very important. Questions must be in boldface type and large enough to be read by a person with or without eyeglasses. The scoring method should be easy for patients to understand and should require little writing. Questions should be worded clearly and should require an objective response from the consumer. The minimum length of questions and the entire questionnaire should be considered. Although ample space should be provided to encourage free-response comments about medical services, patients should not be required to spend a lot of time completing the survey. Space should be provided on the scorecard side of the questionnaire to identify the patient (for the study) and to match scores with appropriate patients. Figure 11.1 shows parts of a scorecard using different formats for responses.

For scoring purposes and for ease of interpretation in preparation for data processing, the inside pages (questions 1-20) require only circles and checks to indicate answers. Although space for comments is provided under the questions, the section for responses is set up to promote uniform scoring procedures and to stand out for easy access by the person recording responses and summarizing them for data analysis. Questions 21 and 22 are answered in a format that permits free response (open-ended comments and remarks). Such answers are generally not applicable for analysis of data that is to include correlations of results. Most often, free responses tell the evaluator about personal biases or opinions of the individual patient, although these opinions can be categorized and grouped for interpretation.

There is a technique that establishes a basis for correlation and other statistical analysis of free responses. Such answers can be quantified by developing a criterion by which to judge a positive from a negative response. Quantifying them (i.e., if a response is

FIGURE 11.1. Sample Questionnaire

Space for Patient I.D. and Related Medical Information		
Please circle the % (50% being average) that corresponds to your level of satisfaction with each of these questions. (If you want to explain answers, use the space after questions.)		
	Negative	**Positive**
1. Were you satisfied with the date and time of your appointment? If not, what could have been done to improve it?	NO 0% 10% 20% 30% 40% 50%	YES 60% 70% 80% 90% 100%
2. Were you given the opportunity to ask questions? _____	NO 0% 10% 20% 30% 40% 50%	YES 60% 70% 80% 90% 100%

Please circle NO or YES. If you want to explain your answer, please use the space following the question.	
	Circle Answer
14. Was this your first visit to the clinic for medical care?	NO YES
15. Was this your first visit to the special service clinic for arthritis?	NO YES
16. Did you receive an appoint-ment to return? If yes, what date(s)? _____ What department(s)? _____	NO YES
17. Did you have any difficulty scheduling appointment(s)? If yes, describe problem(s). _____	NO YES

FIGURE 11.1 *(continued)*

CHECK ANSWER

	Check Your Answer
18. How long did you wait to be seen for your appointment?	1. 0-5 minutes 2. 5-15 minutes 3. 15-30 minutes 4. 30-60 minutes 5. Over one hour
19. Who referred you to the special service clinic for arthritis?	1. Your family doctor 2. Doctor at medical center 3. Nurse 4. Self 5. Other (specify)
20. How many miles from the doctor's office is your residence?	1. Within 20 miles 2. 20-100 miles 3. Over 100 miles

FREE RESPONSE

21. Were there things about your health that you thought were important but were not brought up during your visit to the clinic?

22. Do you have any suggestions or general comments about the service and care received? _____

positive, a 1 is recorded; if it is negative, a 2 is recorded) establishes a basis for statistical analysis. This technique opens the door to determining a variety of relationships between the free response and other results of the evaluation:

- Comparative frequency: count of positive and negative comments
- Tabulation of percentages
- Correlation of comments given (with all the other variables studied), to determine whether comments are becoming increasingly positive or negative at a statistically significant rate
- Prediction of relationships between comments and overall satisfaction

NONCOMPUTERIZED PROCESSING PROCEDURES

Manual System

For small numbers of patients and few requirements of the data, a manual system of recording and summarizing can be used to prepare data for analysis. Data found on the summary for each patient is converted into a grid of numeric scores for all patients on each question (see Figure 11.2). All responses are quantified in the process of conversion, that is, percentages are shown as numbers ranging from 0 to 100; comments are scored dichotomously (1 = positive comments; 2 = negative comments); yes/no responses are scored 1 or 2; and parameters of distance are scored 1, 2, or 3 (1 = living less than 20 miles from doctor's office, 2 = 20-100 miles, and 3 = over 100 miles). Each section of the information is set up for tabulation to summarize average tendencies in a group. In this manner, less-than-favorable opinions about medical services can be made.

A measure of central tendency for the group of patients under study can be derived by dividing the number of respondents into the sum of scores for each question (this will yield the mean average score). In this process, only the actual scores given by each consumer are included in the computational process. This process is sensitive to each score given and represents the satisfaction of the entire group of patients about the service or activity under examination. The more scores available for each question, the more one can be confident that the computed average is an accurate measure of central opinion in the group. Since a score by each consumer for each question is important in the analysis, every attempt must be made to secure all responses. Although it is not absolutely essential to have complete data from each consumer surveyed, the credibility of results may be threatened if sufficient data are missing from the analysis.

Once the average tendency has been determined for each question, it is possible to graph and plot the direction and magnitude of satisfaction from one group to the next, and across all points of evaluation. Missing individual scores interrupts the ability to monitor long-term care management benchmarks on a patient-by-patient basis. Figure 11.3 shows the group average scores from parents of medically needy children provided respite care services.

FIGURE 11.2. Example Grid of Computations for Manual Satisfaction Calculations

| | PARENT QUESTIONNAIRE SCORES | | | | | | | | | | | |
| Subject Number | Rating Questions (0 - 100) | | | | | | | Date | 1 = Yes 2 = No | | Distance 1 = Within 20 miles 2 = 20-100 miles 3 = Over 100 miles | Comments 1 = Positive 2 = Negative |
	1	2	3	4	5	6	7	8	9	10	11	12
001	80	90	100	80	50	100	80		1	2	3	–
002	100	80	90	100	100	0	100		1	1	3	1
003	80	100	100	80	70	50	70		1	2	2	1
004	70	60	60	90	100	50	100		2	1	3	1
005	80	–	–	70	–	–	–		–	–	2	2
006	–	–	80	80	50	50	50		1	2	1	–
007	100	80	–	90	90	–	–		2	1	1	1
008	50	90	60	–	–	90	90		2	1	3	1
009	90	100	–	100	70	–	–		2	1	2	–
010	95	100	90	100	80	70	100		2	1	2	1
011	100	–	90	90	60	100	100		2	1	2	1
TOTALS												
Consumers Responding	10	8	8	10	9	8	8		10	10	11	8
Sum of Scores	845	700	670	880	670	510	690		16	13	24	9
Mean Average Response	84.50	87.50	83.75	88.00	74.44	63.75	86.25		1.60	1.30	2.18	1.13

CASE COORDINATOR QUESTIONNAIRE SCORES

Rating Questions (0 - 100)									Rating (0-100)	Date	1 = Yes 2 = No			Distance 1 = Within 20 miles 2 = 20-100 miles 3 = Over 100 miles	Title	Comments 1 = Positive 2 = Negative
1	2	3	4	5	6	7	8	9	10	11	12	13	14	15	16	17
100	100	100	100	90	80	–	80	70	90				2	2		1
100	100	100	100	90	90	90	100	0	100		2	2	2	3		–
90	90	80	90	80	80	90	80	80	90		2	1	2	2		1
100	90	90	80	90	90	80	100	50	100		2	1	2	2		1
100	100	80	80	90	90	100	100	50	100		2	1	2	2		1
70	90	100	100	90	90	90	90	50	100		2	1	2	2		1
100	80	20	60	20	50	20	80	50	80		2	1	2	3		–
–	–	–	–	–	–	–	–	–	–		–	–	–	–		–
–	–	–	–	–	–	–	–	–	–		–	–	–	–		–
100	100	–	–	–	0	100	–	0	100		2	1	2	2		–
100	100	100	100	100	100	100	100	0	100		2	1	2	1		1
9	9	8	8	8	9	8	8	9	9		9	9	9	9		6
860	850	670	710	650	670	670	730	350	860		18	10	18	19		6
95.55	94.44	83.75	88.75	81.25	74.44	883.75	91.25	38.88	95.55		2.00	1.11	2.00	2.11		1.00

FIGURE 11.3. Respite Care Summary Profiles

Do you feel it would be beneficial to visit the home prior to leaving your child there?

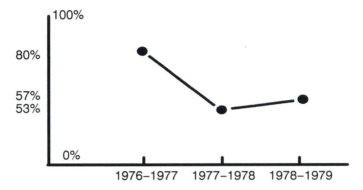

Were you pleased with the overall care provided at the respite care home?

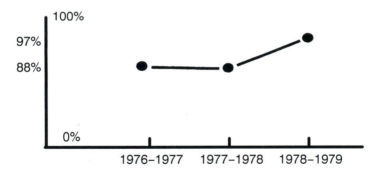

PLANNING FOR COMPUTERIZED SYSTEMS

Needs for comprehensive data associated with large groups or many types of small groups of patients necessitate computerized data processing, storage, and retrieval. For use when entering data, a set of codes and the instructive key describing them is developed. These indicate order and how data to be evaluated are to be coded and in what columns they should appear. The code key for the arrangement of data developed by Sommers is shown in Figure 11.4.[4,6,7,8] A code key is extremely important, since it provides the index by which to interpret the results of data analysis. Make duplicate copies of this instructional sheet, and place them in various files to ensure that one can always be located.

It is possible to obtain both descriptive and inferential information from the same data. Polit and Hungler differentiate between the two forms of analysis.[9] *Descriptive statistics* are used to describe and summarize observations and measurements. Examples include:

- central tendencies or averages (mean, mode, and median), such as the mean birth weight of infants born to mothers addicted to heroin;
- frequencies, such as the frequency or number of subjects who report compliance with instructions for self-medication; and
- percentages, such as the percentage of nursing students who drop out of nursing programs before graduation.

The second broad class of statistical procedures is known as *inferential statistics.* In testing evaluative hypotheses, more than descriptive information is required. For this type of problem, various statistical tests are available that can be classified as inferential. For example, let us assume that we are studying the effects of two types of exercise on heart rates. A sample of fifty adults in good health and good physical condition is used in the study. Twenty-five of these individuals perform exercise A, and twenty-five perform exercise B. Ten minutes after beginning the exercise the heart rates of both groups are measured by taking the radial pulse.

Using descriptive statistics, the average heart rate for the subjects in groups A and B is found to be 91.6 and 101.3, respectively. Can it then be concluded, on the basis of this sample of fifty subjects, that exercise A would increase the heart rate for the entire population of healthy adults less than would exercise B? Might differences in heart rates in the two groups be due to individual variation rather than to an effect of the exercises? Inferential statistics permit us to ascertain the probability that relationships would or would not be replicable with other samples drawn from the same population. In other words, inferential statistics provide an estimate of how reliable our observations may be.

FIGURE 11.4. Code Key of Keypunch Instructions

CARD COLUMNS	QUESTIONS	INSTRUCTIONS
1 - 4	Study Number Assigned To Each Patient	Sequence number at beginning of source sheet —punch leading zeros when less than 1000.
5 - 10	Medical History Code For Patient	Clinic Chart Number
11 - 16	Date of Clinic Visit	Date seen at clinic—punch leading zero when month code is less than 10.
17 - 23	Parent 1 - 7	- = 100% 4 = 40% 9 = 90% 3 = 30% 8 = 80% 2 = 20% 7 = 70% 1 = 10% 6 = 60% 0 = 0% 5 = 50% & = No Response ' (Apostrophe) = Doesn't Apply (N/A)
24 - 25	Parent 8 - 9	1 = Yes; 2 = No; & = No Response ' (Apostrophe) = Doesn't Apply (N/A)
26	Parent 10	1 = 20 miles; 2 = 20-100 miles; 3 = over 100 miles; & = No Response ' (Apostrophe) = Doesn't Apply (N/A)
27	Parent 12	+ = (+); - = (-); 0 = (0); & = No Response
28 - 36	Case Coordinator 1 - 9	- = 100% 4 = 40% 9 = 90% 3 = 30% 8 = 80% 2 = 20% 7 = 70% 1 = 10% 6 = 60% 0 = 0% 5 = 50% & = No Response ' (Apostrophe) = Doesn't Apply (N/A)
37 - 39	Case Coordinator 10 - 12	1 = Yes; 2 = No; & = No Response ' (Apostrophe) = Doesn't Apply (N/A)
40	Case Coordinator 13	- = 100% 4 = 40% 9 = 90% 3 = 30% 8 = 80% 2 = 20% 7 = 70% 1 = 10% 6 = 60% 0 = 0% 5 = 50% & = No Response ' (Apostrophe) = Doesn't Apply (N/A)
41	Case Coordinator 14	1 = 20 miles; 2 = 20-100 miles; 3 = over 100 miles; & = No Response ' (Apostrophe) = Doesn't Apply (N/A)
42	Case Coordinator 15	- = (-); + = (+); 0 = (0); & = No Response
43 - 44	Title of Case Coordinator	PH = Physician PU = Public School Staff HE = Health Nurse DE = Development Disability Staff SO = Social Worker PR = Private Agency UN = Unknown or No Response SE = Self Referral

The examples in Figure 11.5 illustrate descriptive accounts of evaluative information on consumer satisfaction. The data, illustrated as a computer printout, show frequency, breakdown by percentage, and mean average response of consumers to various questions concerning their satisfaction with the service. Each part of the figure represents a different descriptive account. Routine reports of descriptive information, as shown, are obtained at scheduled intervals and are used to monitor consumer input into operations of a program. The data can be stored as a permanent computerized record on mainframe and/or personal computers with adequate memory for future comparisons. Inferential statistical procedures are used to determine significant changes in satisfaction from one evaluative interval to the next, as well as differences between groups in satisfaction with the same service, prediction of future satisfaction that will benefit both consumer and practitioner, and other relationships among specifics in the data, understanding of which can lead to improved medical care and services.[4,7,8]

FIGURE 11.5. Computer Printed Displays of Data (Frequencies, Percentages, and Mean Average Response)

QUESTIONS FOR PARENTS				
WERE YOU GIVEN OPPORTUNITIES TO ASK QUESTIONS?				
Frequency of	87	47.28%	100	Percentage
Consumers with	35	19.02%	90	of Consumers
Same Rating	25	13.59%	80	Making Same
	15	8.15%	70	Rating
	9	4.89%	60	
	5	2.72%	50	Ratings (Scale
	2	1.09%	40	from 1 - 100)
	2	1.09%	30	
	0		20	
	1	.54%	10	
	3	1.63%	0	
	92		no response	
	0		doesn't apply	
Total Number	184	86.09%	mean average response	

FIGURE 11.5 *(continued)*

WERE YOUR APPOINTMENTS SCHEDULED PROPERLY?

97	53.01%	100
24	13.11%	90
23	12.57%	80
10	5.46%	70
6	3.28%	60
12	6.56%	50
3	1.64%	40
3	1.64%	30
1	.55%	20
1	.55%	10
3	1.64%	0
93		no response
0		doesn't apply

Total Number   183   85.25%   mean average response

WERE YOU PLEASED WITH THE OVERALL SERVICE PROVIDED?

77	43.02%	100
29	16.20%	90
27	15.08%	80
14	7.82%	70
5	2.79%	60
17	9.50%	50
2	1.12%	40
1	.56%	30
2	1.12%	20
2	1.12%	10
3	1.68%	0
96		no response
1		doesn't apply

179   82.51%   mean average response

WAS THIS YOUR FIRST VISIT?

112	60.87%	yes
72	39.13%	no
92		no response
0		doesn't apply

DID YOU RECEIVE AN APPOINTMENT TO RETURN?

91	51.12%	yes
87	48.88%	no
98		no response
0		doesn't apply

HOW MANY MILES FROM THE CLINIC DO YOU LIVE?

13	7.10%	20 miles
79	43.17%	20-100 miles
91	49.73%	over 100 miles
93		no response
0		doesn't apply

DO YOU HAVE ANY SUGGESTIONS OR GENERAL COMMENTS ABOUT THE SERVICE AND CARE YOU RECEIVED?

42	49.41%	positive
14	16.47%	negative
29	34.12%	other
191		no response

QUESTIONS FOR CASE COORDINATORS

TITLE OF CASE COORDINATOR

18	6.52%	physician
101	36.59%	public school staff
12	4.35%	health nurse
3	1.09%	developmental disability staff
24	8.70%	social worker
3	1.09%	private agency
30	10.87%	self-referral
85	30.80%	response

WAS THERE ANY EXPLANATION OF THE MEDICAL FINDINGS AS THEY RELATED TO THE EDUCATION OF YOUR CHILD?

65	35.71%	100
26	14.29%	90
27	14.84%	80
25	13.74%	70
7	3.85%	60
16	8.79%	50
4	2.20%	40
3	1.65%	30
3	1.65%	20
3	1.65%	10
3	1.65%	0
94		no response
0		doesn't apply
182	78.63%	mean average response

FIGURE 11.5 *(continued)*

DID YOU RECEIVE A CLEARLY DEVELOPED EXPLANATION OF ALL FINDINGS AFTER YOUR CLINIC VISIT?

59	32.24%	100
24	13.11%	90
32	17.49%	80
14	7.65%	70
7	3.83%	60
21	11.48%	50
2	1.09%	40
4	2.19%	30
3	1.64%	20
6	3.28%	10
11	6.01%	0
93		no response
0		doesn't apply
183	73.17%	mean average response

IS THIS THE FIRST CHILD YOU HAVE REFERRED TO THE CLINIC?

68	36.17%	yes
120	63.83%	no
88		no response
0		doesn't apply

DID YOU RECEIVE A MEDICAL REPORT WITHIN 10 DAYS FOLLOWING THE CHILD'S VISIT?

143	81.25%	yes
33	18.75%	no
99		no response
1		doesn't apply

DID YOU HAVE ANY DIFFICULTY SCHEDULING APPOINTMENTS?

16	8.94%	yes
163	91.06%	no
96		no response
1		doesn't apply

WOULD A PERSONAL VISIT TO YOUR PROGRAM CENTER BY A MEMBER OF OUR STAFF, TO FOLLOW UP ON PROGRESS MADE BY THE CHILD SINCE THE CLINIC VISIT, BE IMPORTANT TO YOU?

27	16.77%	100
14	8.70%	90
15	9.32%	80
6	3.73%	70
7	4.35%	60

28	17.39%	50
5	3.11%	40
2	1.24%	30
5	3.11%	20
14	8.70%	10
38	23.60%	0
111		no response
4		doesn't apply
161	49.07%	mean average response

GENERAL INFORMATION ABOUT CHILDREN UNDER STUDY

192	69.57%	male
84	30.43%	female
		DIAGNOSIS
108	39.13%	learning disability-dyslexia
93	33.70%	hyperactivity
4	1.45%	heart disease
14	5.07%	physical crippling, orthopedic
22	7.97%	hearing disability
14	5.07%	visual disability
94	34.06%	mental/developmental retardation
65	23.55%	emotional-behavioral adjustment RXN
26	9.42%	speech/language disability
20	7.25%	seizures
467	169.20%	other

(Percentages total more than 100; most children served had multiple diagnoses)

AGE GROUPS OF CHILDREN (Average Age 108.36 Months)

1	.36%	0 to 10 months
6	2.17%	11 to 20 months
6	2.17%	21 to 30 months
6	2.17%	31 to 40 months
10	3.62%	41 to 50 months
18	6.52%	51 to 60 months
17	6.16%	61 to 70 months
31	11.23%	71 to 80 months
16	5.80%	81 to 90 months
27	9.78%	91 to 100 months
18	6.52%	101 to 110 months
24	8.70%	111 to 120 months
15	5.43%	121 to 130 months
10	3.62%	131 to 140 months
12	4.35%	141 to 150 months
9	3.26%	151 to 160 months
10	3.62%	161 to 170 months

FIGURE 11.5 *(continued)*

10	3.62%	171 to 180 months
11	3.99%	181 to 190 months
8	3.90%	191 to 200 months
2	.72%	211 to 220 months
4	1.45%	201 to 210 months
2	.72%	221 to 230 months
0		231 to 240 months
0		241 to 250 months
3	1.09%	over 250 months

GROUPING BY DATE OF VISIT

114	41.30%	Group I (7/1/75-6/30/76)
103	37.32%	Group II (7/1/76-1/31/77)
59	21.38%	Group III (2/1/77-7/31/77)
0		Group IV (8/1/77-1/31/78)
0		Group V (2/1/78-7/31/78)
0		Group VI (8/1/78-1/31/79)
0		Group VII (2/1/79-7/31/79)
0		Group VIII (8/1/79-1/31/80)
0		Group IX (2/1/80-7/31/80)
0		Group X (8/1/80-1/31/81)
0		Group XI (2/1/81-7/31/81)
0		Group XII (8/1/81-1/31/82)
0		Group XIII (2/1/82-7/31/82)
0		Group XIV (8/1/82-1/31/83)
0		Group XV (2/1/83-7/31/83)
0		Group XVI (8/1/83-1/31/84)
0		Group XVII (2/1/84-7/31/84)
0		Group XVIII (8/1/84-1/31/85)
0		Group XIX (2/1/85-7/31/85)
0		Group XX (8/1/85-1/31/86)
0		Group XXI (2/1/86-7/31/86)
0		Group XXII (8/1/86-1/31/87)
0		Group XXIII (2/1/87-7/31/87)
0		Group XXIV (8/1/87-1/31/88)
0		Group XXV (2/1/88-7/31/88)

FACTORS TO CONSIDER
WHEN MEASURING SATISFACTION

Who needs to learn what, to effect the most improvement or to maintain excellent services for the patient? And what activities (related to the production of services) account most for consumer satisfaction or dissatisfaction? These are questions basic to the delivery of health care. When addressing these issues, it is helpful to list specific elements associated with the services being provided. Questions are addressed to the consumer about the way specific activities are being performed. If the consumer is less than satisfied, then improvement must be made in the deficient areas. An example of this process is outlined in the following paragraphs. The consumers in this case are two different groups. One group includes parents of handicapped children, and the second is composed of case coordinators (those in the child's home community but outside of their homes, who have responsibility for education, health, or developmental programs for the child). From separate points of view, these groups are asked to evaluate the same service.

Services Offered Parents

- Scheduling appointments
- Providing opportunities to ask questions about all parts of the care provided
- Presenting explanations about all findings
- Presenting explanations of how the results relate to their child's education and development
- Providing individualized evaluation and treatment aimed at increasing the child's progress
- Providing comprehensive service to meet the overall needs of the child and family (beyond the clinical visit, extending into the child's well-being at home, at school, and in the community)
- Exploring need for staff to be sent into the child's home community to follow up on progress

Sample questions for parents can include:

1. Were you given opportunities to ask questions?
2. Was there an explanation of medical findings as they related to the education of your child?

3. Did you receive a clearly developed explanation of all findings after your visit to the doctor?
4. Were your appointments scheduled properly?
5. Has progress been made since your child was seen by the Comprehensive Child Care Center?
6. Would a personal visit to your community by a staff member from the Comprehensive Child Care Center, to follow up on progress made by your child since seeing the doctor, be important to you?
7. Were you pleased with the overall service provided by the Comprehensive Child Care Center?
8. (Group membership by interval): On what date was your child first seen here for his or her exceptional needs?
9. Was this your first visit to the center?
10. Did you receive an appointment to return?
11. Do you have any suggestions or general comments about the service and care you received?

Services Offered Case Coordinators

- Scheduling appointments
- Answering questions about the child's medical evaluation
- Differentiating between the child's medical and nonmedical needs
- Developing specific recommendations for educational programming for the child, in light of the child's health condition
- Clarifying an understanding about status of health in relationship to the child's handicap
- Suggesting therapies to be used at home in the plan for the child's treatment/remediation that are appropriate to resources of the local program and community
- Providing individualized evaluation and treatment aimed at increasing the child's progress
- Assisting local program staff in the development of a plan to be implemented in the home community following intervention by the health service
- Providing necessary help to deal with the child's handicapping conditions

- Sending staff from the health care service into the case coordinator's community to follow up on progress being made by the child
- Providing comprehensive service to meet the overall needs of the case coordinator for this child, which may go beyond medical care and include help in setting the stage for improving the child's life at home and in school
- Providing a complete written report of findings and recommendations within ten days of the visit to the doctor

Sample questions for case coordinators can include:

1. Were the questions you had regarding the medical evaluation of this child answered by staff at the Comprehensive Child Care Center?
2. Was a distinction made between the medical and nonmedical needs of the child?
3. Were the medical findings helpful in determining specific activities of educational programming for the child?
4. Did the medical findings clarify your understanding of this child's exceptional educational needs?
5. Were suggestions made by staff at the Comprehensive Child Care Center (concerning the child's educational activities) appropriate to the resources of your program and community?
6. Did you assist clinical staff in the development of a plan to be used when the child returned home from the clinical visit?
7. Has progress been made since this child was seen by the Comprehensive Child Care Center?
8. Did you receive all assistance from staff at the Comprehensive Child Care Center necessary to deal with the child's exceptional educational needs?
9. Would a personal visit to your program center by a staff member from the Comprehensive Child Care Center, to follow up on progress made by the child since seeing the doctor, be important to you?
10. Were you pleased with the overall service provided by the Comprehensive Child Care Center?
11. (Group membership; see Figure 11.5 for grouping by date of visit): On what date was this child first seen at this clinic?

12. Is this the first child you have referred to the Center?
13. Did you receive a medical report within ten days following the child's visit to this clinic?
14. Did you have any difficulty scheduling appointments here?
15. How far do you live from the center (in miles)?
16. List your professional title: (physician, public school staff, nurse, staff serving developmental disability, social worker, other).
17. Do you have any suggestions or general comments about the care and the service you received?

The questions that a health care provider can ask consumers about their satisfaction with services may vary a great deal. A solo practice is organized differently from practices in a university health service or a multispecialty medical group. It must be kept in mind that questions need to determine how well consumer needs are being met but designed to achieve the goals and objectives of the staff providing the health service.

FORMAT FOR THE ANALYSIS

A review of answers to the questions will identify less than favorable service. If poor ratings or negative comments are noted, a follow-up telephone call to the consumer may be needed to get to the bottom of the problem. It is important to resolve issues as they are identified, to prevent a problem that was initially minor from developing into a major or chronic concern that may affect services to many patients. Further summarization of information from individual questionnaires sets the stage for an examination of the medical care system. The compilation, analysis, and interpretation of quantified, grouped data at systematic intervals provides a format for the location of deficiencies in the system.

PROCEDURES FOR DESCRIPTIVE ANALYSIS OF DATA, WITH ILLUSTRATIONS

Longitudinal measurement of satisfaction with a particular service can be monitored and projected to determine the magnitude and direction of tendencies in the ratings. Illustrations from past examples of various studies follow. For example, a question in the parents' questionnaire assessing multispecialty pediatric services for exceptional children asks: "Did you receive a clearly developed explanation of all findings, after your visit to the clinic?" Mean average ratings of satisfaction for this question, given by seven different groups of parents from 1975 to 1979, were recorded in the following order: 71, 79, 77, 77, 85, and 82 percent. The ratings are displayed in Figure 11.6 as a visual profile.

Visual Displays and Line Graphs

Visually displayed information projects an instant view of satisfaction across many points. If an unsatisfactory rating is noted or an unsatisfactory trend begins to develop, it is necessary to examine those activities responsible for the unsatisfactory service. The visual profile can illustrate the magnitude (by rating percentage) and direction of the trend (positive or negative). Staff must review the

FIGURE 11.6. Trends in Satisfaction Data

Did you receive a clearly developed explanation of all findings after your clinic visit?

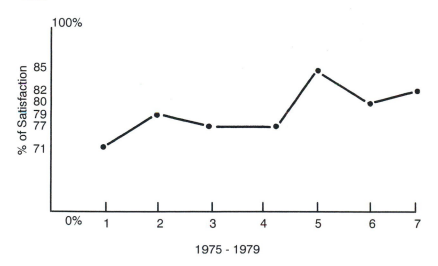

1975 - 1979

specific activities involved in less than satisfactory services to determine the reasons for the deficiencies.

In the example, steps were taken to increase satisfaction associated with the last question (Figure 11.6) to parents. These included:

1. Determining what specific questions each parent wanted to have answered about their child's health care needs (the questions may have been written down or given orally).
2. Reviewing the notes on progress in each child's medical record for the day's service was provided and identifying whether the information presented answered the questions.
3. Determining whether (and by whom) a clearly developed, follow-up, summarizing report explaining all findings was sent.

This reviewing process uncovered the following findings. Poor ratings consistently occurred when (1) the parents failed to state specific questions about the medical and associated health care needs of their child; (2) notes by the physician on the child's progress did not address the parents' questions; or (3) parents did not receive a summarizing report of findings and recommendations, either during or after their visit to the doctor's office.

Figure 11.6 shows a group of ratings of satisfaction before analysis, following analysis, and after modifications were made to correct weaknesses in the system for delivering care. Improved ratings occurred after the fourth evaluative interval, when emphasis was maintained on (1) requiring parents of handicapped children to specify their questions in writing, (2) examining notes on medical progress in light of parents' questions, to make sure the parents' concerns were addressed during the medical evaluation; and (3) confirming that the child's physician or a health care coordinator had sent a summarized follow-up report of findings and recommendations to the parents shortly after the visit to the doctor's office.

Bar Graphs

A sample question shown in Figure 11.7 (from a questionnaire on cleft lip and palate clinic services for children) has drawn patient satisfaction ratings of 51, 73, and 73 percent. Looking at parents'

FIGURE 11.7. Bar Graph—Cleft Lip and Palate

Has progress been made since your child was seen by the cleft lip and palate team?

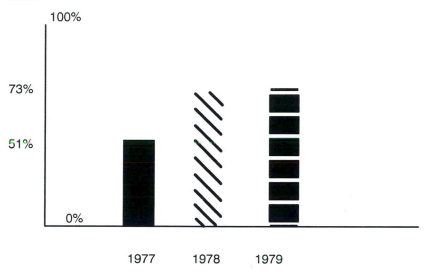

satisfaction with medical respite care services for severely handicapped children finds ratings of 92, 91, and 98 percent for the question in Figure 11.8: "Were the respite care parents warm and receptive to your child?" Ratings are visually profiled in the figure.

Other Applications

The system can be adapted to evaluate and monitor other programs and services. For example, the procedure was applied to a program for access by telephone to taped consultations giving information on health.[10] A special set of questions was developed in postcard format. A brochure illustrating available taped messages focusing on concerns of childhood and adolescence was developed and contained the postcard with questions on consumer satisfaction. After they called a taped message, consumers were asked to fill out and mail in the prestamped, self-addressed postcard evaluating their satisfaction with the information received. Since the names of callers were not requested or given, the procedure remained confidential. Both the age and sex of the caller were obtained, however,

FIGURE 11.8. Bar Graph—Respite Care

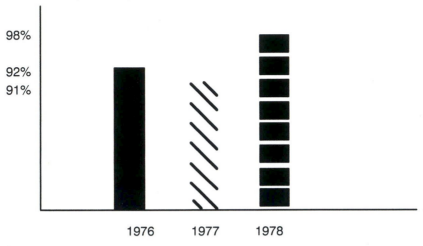

Were the respite care parents warm and receptive to your child?

along with the time the call was made. Using the same procedure for rating consumer satisfaction, results from the program of taped consultations on health information are shown in Figure 11.9.

Some of the free responses and suggestions given on the evaluating forms indicated that consumers wanted more topics for older adolescents, more detailed discussions about the use and abuse of alcohol, clarification of a "fuzzy" tape (could it be recorded in a clearer voice?), addition of a section on alternatives to abortion, and so forth.

Another application of the procedure was in a group counseling session provided for adolescents with tics (neurologically based disorders of movement called Tourette's syndrome).[11] Questions were addressed to these adolescents (boys and girls) following each counseling session, to learn their satisfaction with the activity and to identify topics to be included in future sessions. Results of the survey are illustrated in Figure 11.10.

FORMAT FOR INFERENTIAL ANALYSIS OF DATA, WITH ILLUSTRATIONS

The previous section showed examples of descriptive results. Those who use descriptive statistics want to talk about the data in hand,

FIGURE 11.9. Evaluation Summary of Consumer Satisfaction—Dial Harmony

	Number	Mean Age
1978	6 (5)	24
1979	12 (10)	20

( ) = Female

Key:
June to August 1978 =

March to December 1979 =

Please circle the % (50% being average) that corresponds to your level of satisfaction with each of the following questions:

1. Was the message easy to understand?

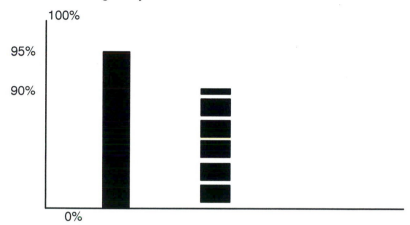

2. Did the information meet your expectations?

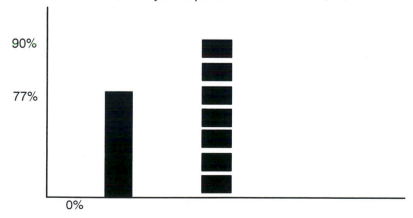

FIGURE 11.9 *(continued)*

3. If you tried an idea suggested, was it successful?

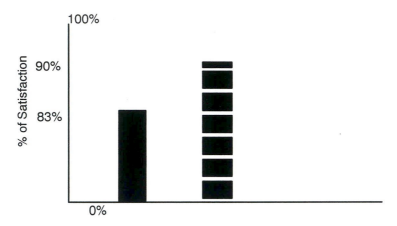

FIGURE 11.10. Group with Tourette's Syndrome—Results of Survey

Rate each question as it corresponds to your level of satisfaction. Circle the percentage (%) that you believe to be most appropriate. A rating of 50% is considered average. A rating above 50% indicates a favorable (positive) response, and a rating below 50% indicates a negative (less than favorable) response.

Example:
NEGATIVE   POSITIVE
NO   YES

| 0% | 10% | 20% | 30% | 40% | 50% | 60% | 70% | 80% | 90% | 100% |

Average Number Responding = 22

Average Rates
of Response,
per Group

Questions

		Average Rates of Response, per Group
1.	Did you enjoy talking about Tourette's with others?	88%
2.	Were all questions you had about Tourette's answered?	55%
3.	Were you given opportunities to ask questions?	82%
4.	Do you feel better about yourself after having participated in the discussion?	92%
5.	Would you like to have another meeting with the same group?	100%

Section for Comments/Suggestions

If another meeting is planned, what would you like to do?
A. Find out what causes Tourette's.
B. Discuss ways of handling inappropriate behavior and ways to stop or handle teasing
C. Be informed of ways to help teachers and students understand Tourette's.
D. Find out how other people cope with it.

which describe current performance.[12] Inferential analysis supplements the evaluative process by providing inferences about trends implied in the data.[13] Statistical knowledge is added to descriptions of trends in satisfaction, to help minimize error (variance) and identify more precisely those activities that may be related to less than favorable ratings and comments.[6,8,14]

Longitudinal Study

As questionnaires on satisfaction are sent to new groups of consumers at scheduled intervals, current ratings are compared to past ratings to determine the direction (positive or negative) and the magnitude (percentage) of change. Statistical processes are applied to the data to determine which services need modification to help them become more satisfactory to consumers. Once identified, activities of primary importance are increased for maximum benefit to the patient (and parent, if the patient is a child), thus leading to improved care and services and increased satisfaction. Analysis of evaluative data obtained at scheduled collecting intervals enables staff to determine the appropriateness of modifications.

The procedure was applied to data on consumer satisfaction obtained from medical services provided to handicapped children (N = 402) between July 1, 1975 and July 31, 1978[7] and to other groups of handicapped children (N = 152) served from August 1, 1978 to July 31, 1979.[2] The goal of this procedure was to examine findings from different groups of consumers of the same system for delivering services. Similarities and differences were compared in an attempt to determine predictable patterns and relationships. Parents and case coordinators completed questionnaires that contained questions in the first part reflecting ratings of satisfaction with services (on a scale of 1 to 100 percent), while questions in the second part elicited dichotomous (yes/no) answers, checked answers, or free responses. The top panels of Tables 11.1 and 11.2 reflect ratings by parents and case coordinators over the years, while the bottom panels present answers to questions not about rating satisfaction. Procedures for analysis of variance (ANOVA) were performed on the data to determine whether rating changes were occurring at a statistically significant rate (p = 0.05).

TABLE 11.1 Parent Questionnaire

Part A. Parent evaluation ratings comparison

Questions answered on a rating scale (1 - 100)	Mean average rating							ANOVA				
	1/7/75 to 6/30/76	1/7/76 to 1/31/77	1/2/77 to 7/31/77	1/8/77 to 1/31/78	1/2/78 to 7/31/78	1/8/78 to 1/31/79	1/2/79 to 7/31/79	X	SEM	N	F ratio	P value
1. Were you given opportunities to ask questions?	84.20 (90)	87.70 (53)	88.10 (41)	88.70 (38)	88.80 (51)	88.90 (47)	89.10 (40)	87.50	0.97	360	0.66	0.68
2. Was there an explanation of the medical findings as they related to the education of your child?	75.50 (89)	83.70 (52)	79.00 (41)	80.30 (38)	80.80 (51)	79.20 (47)	86.10 (38)	80.00	1.28	356	1.14	0.34
3. Did you receive a clear explanation of all findings after your clinic visit?	70.50 (89)	74.90 (53)	76.80 (41)	76.10 (38)	82.90 (52)	80.00 (47)	85.30 (40)	77.10	1.48	360	1.95	0.07
4. Were your appointments scheduled properly?	89.30 (90)	80.40 (52)	82.40 (41)	82.60 (38)	87.50 (51)	87.40 (46)	88.30 (40)	85.90	1.18	358	1.33	0.24
5. Has progress been made since your child was seen by the Comprehensive Child Care Center?	68.70 (87)	64.40 (50)	67.00 (39)	71.80 (38)	66.20 (50)	69.60 (46)	68.10 (36)	67.90	1.56	346	0.31	0.93
6. Would a personal visit to your community by a member of the Comprehensive Child Care Center to follow up on progress made by your child since the clinic visit be important to you?	57.30 (81)	56.00 (47)	55.00 (40)	57.50 (36)	57.50 (50)	50.50 (43)	58.70 (37)	56.20	2.10	334	0.22	0.97
7. Were you pleased with the overall service provided by the Comprehensive Child Care Center?	82.10 (87)	84.00 (51)	82.00 (41)	86.40 (36)	85.80 (52)	83.60 (47)	84.80 (40)	83.80	1.19	354	0.30	0.94

Part B. Additional information

8. Group membership (defined by the time interval the child was first seen for his or her exceptional needs).
9. Is it your first visit to the center?
10. Did you receive an appointment to return?
11. How far do you live from the center (in miles)?
12. Do you have any suggestions or general comments about the service and care you received?

( ) = Number responding to that question.

Source: Sommers, PA. Multivariate analysis applied to the delivery of medical services: a focus on evaluation and replication, *International Journal of Applied Psychology*, 34(2), pp. 203-224. Copyright 1985 by Sage Publications, Inc. Reprinted by Permission of Sage Publications, Inc.

TABLE 11.2. Case Coordinator Questionnaire

Part A. Case coordinator evaluation ratings comparison

Questions answered on a rating scale (0 - 100)	Mean average rating							ANOVA				
	1/7/75 to 6/30/76	1/7/76 to 1/31/77	1/2/77 to 7/31/77	1/8/77 to 1/31/78	1/2/78 to 7/31/78	1/8/78 to 1/31/79	1/2/79 to 7/31/79	X	SEM	N	F ratio	P value
1. Were the questions you had regarding the medical evaluation of this child answered by Comprehensive Child Care Center staff?	74.20 (90)	74.00 (55)	78.80 (41)	81.90 (36)	81.00 (41)	82.60 (46)	84.00 (45)	78.60	1.11	354	2.11	0.05
2. Was a distinction made between the medical and nonmedical needs of the child?	72.80 (89)	72.70 (55)	77.60 (41)	69.50 (37)	78.20 (39)	82.50 (44)	83.80 (45)	76.20	1.14	350	2.98	0.00
3. Were the medical findings helpful in determining specific educational programming activities for the child?	66.90 (88)	62.00 (55)	68.70 (38)	71.10 (38)	72.30 (39)	78.20 (44)	76.50 (43)	70.00	1.36	345	2.53	0.02
4. Did the medical findings clarify your understanding of the child's exceptional educational needs?	67.60 (88)	67.20 (54)	70.50 (38)	73.50 (37)	74.10 (39)	78.00 (44)	72.20 (44)	71.20	1.37	344	1.21	0.30
5. Were suggestions made by Comprehensive Child Care Center staff concerning the child's educational activities appropriate to your program activities and community resources?	61.10 (86)	65.90 (54)	63.90 (41)	69.70 (37)	75.80 (38)	78.00 (45)	73.30 (43)	68.50	1.40	344	3.35	0.00
6. Did you assist clinic staff in the development of a plan to be used when the child returned home from the clinic visit?	35.40 (83)	45.00 (52)	32.40 (38)	39.00 (38)	54.40 (34)	54.70 (45)	42.00 (46)	42.30	1.97	336	2.68	0.01
7. Has progress been made since child was seen by the Comprehensive Child Care Center?	63.20 (87)	67.70 (53)	62.30 (39)	71.80 (39)	67.60 (33)	73.30 (45)	66.70 (42)	67.00	1.38	338	1.27	0.27
8. Did you receive all necessary assistance from Comprehensive Child Care Center staff to deal with the child's exceptional educational needs?	62.50 (85)	65.90 (53)	66.50 (40)	69.00 (38)	70.80 (33)	76.70 (44)	78.00 (45)	69.00	1.40	343	2.70	0.01
9. Would a personal visit to your program center by a member of the Comprehensive Child Care Center to follow up on progress made by the child since the clinic visit be important to you?	53.20 (78)	40.20 (48)	52.40 (34)	40.80 (38)	52.40 (33)	42.00 (44)	33.00 (45)	45.30	2.03	320	2.22	0.04
10. Were you pleased with the overall service provided by the Comprehensive Child Care Center?	74.10 (83)	71.20 (52)	74.90 (41)	78.50 (39)	82.10 (39)	86.30 (46)	89.20 (47)	79.00	1.13	347	5.53	0.00

TABLE 11.2 *(continued)*

Part B. Additional information

11. Group membership (see Table 11.1).
12. Is this the first child you've referred to the center?
13. Did you receive a medical report within ten days following the child's visit?
14. Did you have any difficulty scheduling appointments?
15. How far do you live from the center (in miles)?
16. The title of case coordinator (physician, public school staff, health nurse, developmental disability staff, social worker).
17. Do you have any suggestions or general comments about the service and care you received?

( ) = Number responding to that question.

Source: Sommers, PA. Multivariate analysis applied to the delivery of medical services: a focus on evaluation and replication, *International Journal of Applied Psychology*, 34(2), pp. 203-224. Copyright 1985 by Sage Publications, Inc. Reprinted by Permission of Sage Publications, Inc.

Ratings by Parents

Parents' ratings on all questions showed very positive, stable increases in satisfaction. Since ratings on a majority of the questions (1, 2, 3, 4, and 7) were at a fairly high (80 percent or more) level of satisfaction in the study,[7] the potential was diminished for demonstrating statistically significant gains over the last year of the study. In 1978, the results of a similar study had confirmed that parents' satisfaction with overall medical services was significantly higher than case coordinators' satisfaction ($p = 0.05$).[6] A primary reason for this statistical difference was believed to be the personal contact afforded parents while at the doctor's office. This contact allowed parents to become personally acquainted with the doctor and the staff, thus facilitating resolution of problems and clarification of any questions at the time of the office visit. Parents had maintained a rather high rating of satisfaction from the beginning of the study in 1975, and their ratings will probably not go much higher (law of diminishing returns). To keep ratings as high as possible, however, specific emphasis is placed on activities associated with statistically significant questions, such as providing parents with ample opportunity to ask questions, developing clear explanations of clinical findings, scheduling appropriate and efficient appointments, and striving for optimal progress for each patient. The reasons for emphasizing each of these activities are discussed in the subsection, "Advanced Analysis: Predicting Consumer Satisfaction" (see Table 11.3 for parent results and Table 11.4 for case coordinator results).

Ratings by Case Coordinators

A majority of questions demonstrated significant gains in case coordinators' satisfaction from 1975 to 1979. The increase was statistically significant ($p = 0.05$) on questions 1-3, 5, 6, and 8-10. Very positive, stable gains were reflected for the remaining questions (4 and 7). To promote these increases, major emphasis had been placed on the following activities referred to in the questions: transmitting medical information to case coordinators in language appropriate for determining specific educational activities for the handicapped child; clearly answering all questions about the child's visit to the doctor; clarifying medical and nonmedical needs of the

TABLE 11.3. Prediction of Primary Medical Targets by Parents

Primary target	Consumer variables associated with prediction of primary target	
	1975 - 1978 (N = 402)	1978 - 1979 (N = 554)
Overall pleasure with services (Question 7)	Question 1 — rating of opportunity to ask questions. Question 3 — rating of how clear the explanation of clinic findings was made to parents. Question 5 — rating of progress made by child following medical intervention. Question 4 — rating of how well appointments were scheduled. Overall R^2 = 76%	Question 2 — rating of explanation of medical findings related to education of child. Question 1 — rating of opportunity to ask questions. Question 4 — rating of how well appointments were scheduled. Question 3 — rating of how clear the explanation of clinic findings was made to parents. Question 5 — rating of progress by child since medical intervention. Question 6 — rating of need for staff to visit child in home community. Overall R^2 = 46%
Progress made following medical intervention (Question 5)	Question 7 — rating of overall pleasure with services. Question 8 — group membership (time interval child was seen). Overall R^2 = 24%	Question 7 — rating of overall pleasure with services. Overall R^2 = 9%
Free response comments made about services	Question 7 — rating of overall pleasure with services. Overall R^2 = 69%	Question 7 — rating of overall pleasure with services. Question 3 — rating of how clear the explanation of clinic findings was made to parents. Overall R^2 = 71%

Source: Sommers, PA. Multivariate analysis applied to the delivery of medical services: A focus on evaluation and replication, International Journal of Applied Psychology. 34(2), pp. 203-224. Copyright 1985 by Sage Publications, Inc. Reprinted by Permission of Sage Publications, Inc.

Notes: Variables are presented in the order of their entrance into the stepwise regression equations. Questions are cross-referenced with Table 11.1. Only consumer variables with P value for entry in the equation greater than 0.05 are included.

TABLE 11.4. Prediction of Primary Medical Targets by Case Coordinators

Primary target	Consumer variables associated with prediction of primary target	
	1975 - 1978 (N = 402)	1978 - 1979 (N = 554)
Overall pleasure with services (Question 7)	Question 3 — rating of how helpful medical findings were in determining specific educational activities for child. Question 1 — rating of how well staff answered questions based upon child's visit. Overall R^2 = 70%	Question 1 — rating of how well staff answered questions based upon child's clinic visit. Question 3 — rating of how helpful medical findings were in determining specific educational activities for child. Question 8 — rating of how well staff provided all necessary assistance. Question 11 — group membership (time interval child was seen). Question 5 — rating of how appropriate staff suggestions were to local programs and resources. Question 2 — rating of distinction made between medical and nonmedical needs of child. Question 13 — was medical report received in ten days following clinic visit? Overall R^2 = 71%
Progress made following medical intervention (Question 7)	Question 3 — rating of how helpful medical findings were in determining specific educational activities for child. Question 2 — rating of distinction made between medical and nonmedical needs of child. Question 5 — rating of how appropriate staff suggestions were to local programs and resources. Question 12 — first child referred to center. Overall R^2 = 62%	Question 8 — rating of how well staff provided all necessary assistance. Question 15 — distance coordinator lives from center (in miles). Question 5 — rating of how appropriate staff suggestions were to local programs and resources. Question 12 — first child referred to center. Question 11 — group membership (time interval child was seen). Question 6 — rating of how much assistance case coordinator provided clinic staff in development of follow-up plan. Overall R^2 = 31%
Free response comments made about services	Question 10 — rating of overall pleasure with services. Question 7 — rating of progress made by child following medical intervention. Question 15 — distance coordinator lives from center (in miles). Question 8 — rating of how well staff provided all necessary assistance. Overall R^2 = 78%	Question 10 — rating of overall pleasure with services. Question 7 — rating of progress made by child following medical intervention. Question 14 — difficulty scheduling appointments. Overall R^2 = 76%

Source: Sommers, P.A. Multivariate analysis applied to the delivery of medical services: A focus on evaluation and replication. *International Journal of Applied Psychology*, 34(2), pp. 203-224. Copyright 1985 by Sage Productions, Inc. Reprinted by Permission of Sage Publications, Inc.

Notes: Variables are presented in the order of their entrance into the stepwise regression equations. Questions are cross-referenced with Table 11.2. Only consumer variables with *P* value for entry in the equation greater than 0.05 are included.

child; providing verbal and written reports about the evaluation and treatment plan that could be easily integrated into the child's learning program; and encouraging doctors and staff to provide all necessary assistance to the child and the family throughout the evaluation and follow-up.

Comparisons Among Groups

It might be asked, "Are there statistically significant differences among ratings of satisfaction given by various groups of consumers of the same service?" Some services may be received by groups who, by themselves, may not be able to respond accurately to consumer-oriented questions; many handicapped children fall into this category. Since the child's parents have vested interests in the services received, they are consumer advocates on behalf of their children. Second, by law (PL 94-142), the public school district in which the child resides has responsibilities for educational assessment and programming; social service agencies and public health and other related supportive service organizations are also required to comply with the law in meeting the needs of this group. Once they have undertaken those responsibilities, staff from these agencies and organizations have frequent occasion to refer such children to medical facilities for evaluation and treatment; they may then act as case coordinators for the child at the local level.

An assessment of consumer satisfaction in such cases would focus on an analysis of differences between two different groups in their opinions of services provided to the same child. Figure 11.11 depicts the results of an analysis of the differences between these groups in their answers on three identical questions found in both questionnaires (parents' and case coordinators').[6] Check for discrepancies between opinions of parents and of case coordinators on the same items on each questionnaire.

A matched-pair analysis was made of the differences in responses from parents and case coordinators. Only findings from the question "Were you pleased with the overall service provided by the Comprehensive Child Care Center?" yielded a significant difference. This suggests that careful attention should be given to the values of both groups, if ratings similar to those in the example are anticipated. The

FIGURE 11.11. Discrepancy Check Between Parent and Case Coordinator Questionnaires

Questions	1/7/75 to 6/30/76		1/7/76 to 6/30/77	
	No. of matched pairs responding	T value	No. of matched pairs responding	T value
Has progress been made since your child was seen by the Comprehensive Child Care Center?	66	1.03 ns	56	-0.99 ns
(Question 5 for parents, 7 for case coordinators.)				
Would a personal visit to your community by a member of the Comprehensive Child Care Center to follow up on progress made by your child since seeing the doctor be important to you?	59	-0.09 ns	52	1.68 ns
(Question 6 for parents, 9 for case coordinators.)				
Were you pleased with the overall service provided by the Comprehensive Child Care Center?	64	2.95*		2.09*
(Question 7 for parents, 13 for case coordinators.)				

ns = not significant at 0.05.
* = significant at 0.05.

Source: Sommers, P.A. Multivariate analysis applied to the delivery of medical services: A focus on evaluation and replication, *International Journal of Applied Psychology*, 34(2), pp. 203-224. Copyright 1985 by Sage Publications, Inc. Reprinted by Permission of Sage Publications, Inc.

difference in overall perception may mean that parents and case coordinators have different expectations of the services delivered to a child during and following the medical intervention.

Perhaps providers of health services should identify the differing needs of parents and case coordinators and make sure that services are provided to meet the individual needs of both groups. Findings statistically significant at one point in time may change by the end of the next period of evaluation. Figure 11.11 showed a significant difference in ratings by parents and by case coordinators of satisfaction with overall service provided by staff (p = 0.05). When this statistical test was repeated the following year with new groups of parents and case coordinators, a similar result occurred. Longitudinal evaluation of subsequent ratings of consumer satisfaction can determine the success of the system in meeting their needs.

Advanced Analysis: Predicting Consumer Satisfaction

The delivery of a specific medical service, for example, a pediatric neurological assessment to rule out or confirm a condition such as epilepsy, requires a coordinated series of activities by the doctor, the staff, and laboratory personnel. It involves the scheduling of appointments, collection of background information, providing patients the opportunity to ask questions, explaining findings in light of a child's needs, recommending appropriate therapies, sending a written report of findings to those authorized (after the child has been evaluated), and checking on progress made by the child after leaving the doctor's office. A fairly standard series of events is included in each child's doctor visit, whether it be for a routine optical examination by one doctor or for multiple appointments with a group of specialists (Figure 11.12). The latter requires development of a coordinated, interdisciplinary plan that integrates all the services. Each service activity is identifiable and can be measured. It is important to recognize the relationship of one step to the next, since it is the combined effect of separate activities that equals the overall production of a complete service.

FIGURE 11.12. Steps in a Visit to a Doctor's Office

Step 1	Step 6
Appointment made	General physical exam by nurse, e.g., weight, blood pressure, temperature, and so on
Step 2	Step 7
Collection of records and other information for registration	Physical exam by doctor
Step 3	Step 8
Checking in at doctor's office and completing required information	Discussion of all results with doctor
Step 4	Step 9
Laboratory and X-ray studies completed	Discussion of treatment plan with doctor
Step 5	Step 10
EEG and/or EKG tests completed	Return home, start plan, and follow-up contact with doctor if needed

This example describes the classification of a patient's visit to the doctor by outlining routine activities that occur in three stages: before, during, and after the office visit. Less than favorable opinions of one or more steps may leave the consumer feeling dissatisfied with the visit in total. Some consumers may excuse poor service at certain steps if the final product meets their overall needs. By asking consumers to rate their satisfaction of both general and specific aspects of the service, it is possible to determine how great a contribution each element makes to the patient's overall opinion. Consumer satisfaction with medical services will change in relation to the emphasis placed upon the delivery of services by physicians and staff. If overall service improves, consumer ratings of individual services will improve. If a specific activity improves, it is predictable that patients' ratings of satisfaction with the activity will improve. At some point, the law of diminishing returns will be reached, and ratings will stabilize at a level (one hopes) acceptable to the practitioner and of maximum benefit to the patient. The task of managing positive change in the system can be monitored statistically through application of advanced inferential analysis.

Predictive Studies

Stepwise multiple linear regression analysis[13] was applied to data in the example to predict which service activities were most important to the following targets: (1) consumer satisfaction with overall medical services, (2) progress perceived by parents and case coordinators to have been made by the child following medical intervention, and (3) comments made about services. Individual predictive analyses of data gathered for these patients (N = 554) are reflected for both parents and case coordinators in Tables 11.3 and 11.4. The most important activities are listed in order of priority. As illustrated in the section labeled 1978-1979 in Tables 11.3 and 11.4, some activities continue to be as important to these groups of consumers as they were in the period 1975 to 1978, while others (of less importance initially) have become more important with the addition of information from new patients.[2]

The increase in numbers of variables useful as predictors for targets related to case coordinators (see Table 11.4) can be accounted for by increased knowledge from the numerous significant gains in ratings. Extremely positive and representative gains occurred across all questions to case coordinators. Therefore, the plan for maintaining and improving satisfaction among case coordinators required that specific time and effort be placed on emphasizing each service activity, rather than on a few, as in 1979. Analysis of data from parents (see Table 11.3) confirmed the continuing importance of the same questions (1, 3, 4, and 5) in predicting overall satisfaction, and of Question 7 in predicting progress following medical intervention and predicting comments. Questions 2 and 6 became more important to overall satisfaction with services and Question 3 more important in eliciting comments. As in the case of the coordinators, parents' satisfaction (on all questions rated) steadily increased.

Interestingly, the parents' rating of progress did not appear to relate to any other question (other than to "overall satisfaction" at a very low correlation, $R^2 = 0.09$). A possible reason could be that parents do not mix their thoughts about perceived progress with the other questions more characteristic of service quality (Table 11.3). This supports a previous contention that parents are primarily interested in their child's health and are more critical of changes (or lack of changes) that may be related to the handicapping condition. If medical intervention cannot remove or diminish the severity of the handicapping condition, it is probable that parental satisfaction with the question will remain at an average level (50 to 70 percent) rather than in a higher range of satisfaction (70 to 100 percent). In the coordinators' case, this phenomenon is not as obvious, which also supports a previous contention. Case coordinators relate a variety of activities with quality in their perception of satisfaction with progress. Progress, to the case coordinator, includes the quality of communication and of general services received during and after intervention, in addition to the usefulness of the medical information back in the child's home community (see Table 11.4).

Chapter 12

Implementing Consumers' Ratings of Satisfaction with Your Practice

PATIENT RELATIONS

How can your medical practice improve interactions with patients and their families and friends to make consumer satisfaction a way of doing business, in a manner acceptable to patients, the medical staff, employees, administration, the board, and the community?

Goal

To implement a program of rating consumer satisfaction that makes excellence a way of doing business in all interactions with patients and their families and friends.

Issues

1. Patients do not receive enough information regarding their condition.
2. Families and friends do not receive enough information regarding the patient's condition.
3. Current communications do not allow feedback from patients.
4. Current scheduling procedures cause excessive waiting times for patients.

Causes

There is a lack of communication among physicians, nonphysician staff, and patients and their families and friends.

Alternative Solutions, Associated Areas of Consideration, and Findings

Implement a formal program of patient education to address patients', families', and visitors' questions regarding the clinic, their condition, their surgery, or all of these. Published studies indicate that the more involvement patients have with their own care, the greater the likelihood of increased consumer satisfaction.

Potential Programs for Patient Education

1. It is essential to actively involve each patient in care planning.
    a. Send personal letters to all patients following treatment to explain proceedings of the visit and restate instructions regarding medication or therapy.
    b. Send specific educational and/or training recommendations to those diagnosed with a particular condition (by common diagnosis).
    c. Allow patient, family, and visitors access to a library containing medical information in lay terms.
    d. Establish closed-circuit television programming for patients, families, and visitors to view special programs regarding their medical conditions and interests.
    e. Allow patients, families, and friends access to videotapes with information regarding their medical interests.
    f. Implement specialized classes on common medical conditions for patients, families, and, if applicable, visitors.
2. Implement surveys of patients, mailed or handed out to them, soliciting feedback regarding the services provided them. Published studies have indicated that encouraging increased feedback increases consumer satisfaction.
3. Maintain a telephone hotline so patients have easy access to medical information.
4. Provide assistance with insurance claims and billing to patients and families. Studies indicate that one of the main sources of consumer dissatisfaction is the inability to gain help with insurance claims and/or billing procedures.

Potential Sources of Help

1. Have a designated person in the billing department available for questions from patients and families.
2. Distribute a telephone number to patients and families that allows access to information regarding insurance claims and billings.
3. Establish focus groups in which active patients are asked to provide feedback to the clinic. Focus groups allow feedback from patients, a key factor in increasing consumer satisfaction.
4. Maintain a log of all complaints by patients, and follow up proceedings on those complaints. A log allows common complaints to be recognized and addressed.
5. Develop new scheduling procedures that recognize the value of patients' time. Studies need to be initiated to determine which patients are likely to cancel appointments or be "no-shows" and the like, in order to develop scheduling procedures that are optimal for physicians and patients.

Medical practices need to address appointment scheduling, communications, the education of patients, families, and visitors, and access to information and help to resolve insurance claims and billing issues in order to begin the process of making consumer satisfaction a way of doing business.

SUPPORT AND INVOLVEMENT OF MANAGEMENT

How can medical practices make consumer satisfaction the way of doing business through the involvement and support of their managers, in a manner acceptable to patients, physicians, employees, administration, the board, and the community? Why is it not now the way of doing business?

Issues

1. Support by top management through voluntary commitment for a consumer satisfaction program is not normally visible to employees or patients.

2. There may not now be a position, at the administrative level, focused on achieving consumer satisfaction.
3. Upper management does not have direct and visible contact with patients.
4. The goals and efforts of a consumer satisfaction program are not communicated and coordinated among departments at the management or operational levels.

Causes

At present, the policy of top management may be to delegate responsibility for consumer satisfaction.

Alternative Solutions

1. According to studies and interviews with managerial professionals, support by top management through voluntary commitment is mandatory for successful implementation of such a program.
2. Top managers must proactively develop and implement the program for increasing consumer satisfaction, integrating it into their way of doing business, starting with voluntary commitment expressed by their own actions.
3. Top managers must have contact with the patients.

Suggested Activities

1. All members of the top managerial team should introduce themselves to one consumer each week and ask about his or her visit to the clinic.
2. Administrators should take turns helping in areas where patients wait. Focus on areas with high volumes of patients such as women's health centers, pediatrics, and adult mental health. The administrators should wear name tags with their titles so that patients know who they are.
3. Top management should choose a champion for the project at the administrative level. Studies say that a champion at the

executive level adds credibility to a consumer satisfaction project and helps build support for it in all departments. A champion will coordinate managerial efforts and can help avoid duplication of efforts.

4. Set up a brainstorming committee for consumer satisfaction consisting of leaders from all departments. These should include but need not be limited to risk management, quality assurance, accounts receivable, public relations, nursing, lab, and medical director.

INPUT FROM AND PARTICIPATION BY EMPLOYEES

How can your clinic make consumer satisfaction a way of doing business through input from and participation by employees, in a manner acceptable to patients, physicians, employees, administration, the board, and the community? A goal can be to improve employee relations.

Solutions

1. Solicit opinions of employees on their working environment, on problems in performing services, and on consumer satisfaction; respond to all their suggestions and concerns immediately. Employee involvement will increase their participation and their "buy-in" to this program. Inexpensive ways to obtain input from employees include:
   a. Surveys of employee opinions, conducted every six months. Surveys must be written so as to retain anonymity. Managers must respond to all suggestions and conclusions. Send results to all employees, administration, and medical staff.
   b. Focus groups of employees, conducted monthly. Include these work groups in the plan for the program for improved service. Implement these groups immediately, to develop criteria for performance of services, from the standards and expectations of those on the job.
   c. Staff meetings, conducted with department heads, supervisors, and line employees. Encourage input and suggestions for improving consumer satisfaction at your clinic.

    d. Implement a widely promoted and responsive program for a suggestion box. Top management should send out a letter asking for input, and should personally read the suggestions. It may be that management is currently seen as having a closed-door policy.

2. Recognize "heroes" in the provision of quality service, with dramatic awards such as vacation days or cash bonuses. Your clinic might nominate a Pro of the Month, who is taken out to lunch with the clinic president, given a plaque and a gift (e.g., free meal tickets for a month). This type of program is good at signaling change in the culture, but it is not an incentive strong enough for employees to change behavior over the long term. Limit the award to four times a year so that the program will not become watered down and lose credibility, but employees will not forget it; the following year, reduce the award to semiannually.

3. Translate criteria for performance into job descriptions, and make it a substantial part of performance reviews and considerations for raises in pay.

4. Revising job descriptions and performance reviews becomes part of the agenda of the consumer service program; it must get top priority, in order not to slow completion.

5. Training sessions must be tailored specifically for each department, focusing on employees in positions with high public contact such as nurses, receptionists, and account representatives. When training and educational sessions are voluntary, employees should still be held responsible (in reviews) for their consumer satisfaction skills. Voluntary training may not provide a strong enough incentive to change behavior and may result in inconsistent patterns of service. Studies say mandatory participation is most effective. Include in training sessions tapes of patients' focus groups. This can be an effective review of their performance, but it is essential to maintain confidentiality of patients' results. Department managers should be trained so that they encourage and reinforce desired behavior in consumer relations.

QUALITY ASSURANCE AND RISK MANAGEMENT

How can consumer satisfaction with your clinic be increased through the use of quality assurance and risk management? What is the current approach in these areas?

Issues

1. Departments dealing with quality assurance and risk management may not currently be involved at appropriate levels in focusing on consumer satisfaction.
2. It may be that some malpractice cases are filed because patients lack information, not because the treatment lacked quality.
3. The medical staff may not be fully aware of the impact of low consumer satisfaction on the filing of malpractice suits.

Causes

Quality assurance and risk management may not have been recognized throughout the medical practice as potential ways to increase consumer satisfaction.

Alternative Solutions

1. Involve the quality committee in the development of the definition and standards for a consumer satisfaction program at your clinic. Quality of care is essential. The quality committee might contribute to surveys to help increase patient satisfaction.
2. Implement programs for patient education. Patients are less likely to be dissatisfied with the quality of care if they are given information regarding their medical condition and the corresponding treatment.
3. Implement programs to educate the medical staff about patient satisfaction. Patients are less likely to be dissatisfied with care or to file malpractice claims when the doctor implements a "high touch" form of care, and when the physician provides information regarding the patient's condition or treatment.

Chapter 13

Quality Redefined

In the pursuit of excellence one must:

- Care beyond what others think is wise,
- Envision more than most feel is practical,
- Chance beyond what others see as safe, and
- Anticipate more than others think is possible.

adapted verse by M. R. Mittelstadt, 1990

EXCELLENCE IS EVERYTHING

Quality is the target of both clinical and service excellence in health care today. Although providers and related care giving facilities, services, and programs have established standards of practice, the ultimate determiner of quality is a total voluntary commitment by providers to embrace patient-focused care. Combine this fact with the reality that it is the consumer's perception which totally determines the degree of excellence or quality.

Quality assurance organizations help to formalize policies and procedures for providers and health care systems. Accreditation requirements have added safeguards to ensure and preserve the highest level of care and treatment for each patient. In this regard, a shift is occurring toward patient-focused systems founded on continuous quality improvement.[1] Accreditation by the Joint Commission on Accreditation of Healthcare Organizations (JCAHO) gradually is moving its focus from assurance of good quality service to improvement of quality.[2] Improvement of outcomes for the patient,

177

the enhancement of organizational responsibility, and the implementation of principles for continuous quality improvement are moving to the forefront of JCAHO activity. The Joint Commission is a not-for-profit organization that performs accreditation reviews primarily on hospitals, other institutional facilities, and outpatient facilities. Most managed care plans require any hospital under contract to be accredited by the Joint Commission.[3]

The National Committee for Quality Assurance (NCQA) is a private not-for-profit organization that assesses and reports on managed care plans on several levels. The information on accreditation that the NCQA provides is intended to enable purchasers and consumers of managed care to distinguish among plans based on quality. The NCQA is the leading accrediting body for managed care plans, as well as for some of the performance measures used today.[4] It evaluates how well health plans manage all parts of their delivery system—physicians, hospitals, other providers, and administrative services—in order to continuously improve health care for their members.

The Accreditation Association for Ambulatory Health Care (AAAHC) primarily accredits ambulatory surgery centers, although it has accredited several managed care plans using two groups of standards that are applied as appropriate. Core standards apply to and include rights of patients, governance structure, administration, quality of care provided, quality management and improvement (which includes peer review, quality improvement, and risk management), clinical records, professional improvement, and facilities and environment.[5]

QUALITY, CONSUMER SATISFACTION, AND THE PRACTICE OF MEDICINE

Cast aside what is thought to be the patient's need and instead ask the patient about his or her expectations. Once the expectations have been defined, it is up to the physician and supporting staff to fulfill them.[6] Best defined as perception, consumer satisfaction is a style, a total quality experience, a voluntary commitment by providers to deliver health care and achieve excellence. Health care is primarily a physician-driven service. Without the commitment, leadership, and follow-through of physicians in the area of consumer satisfaction, little (if any) progress can be sustained. It is essential, therefore, that physicians take a leading and active role in identifying and implementing the changes needed to make consumer satisfaction a way of doing business in hospitals and medical practices. By caring enough about their patients to make these changes, physicians will find that their patients will remain loyal and will return to them whenever they have a health care problem.

Patients Differentiate Quality by the Nature of Care and Treatment Received

For physicians to thrive instead of just survive in the contemporary marketplace, traditional approaches to achieve excellence in medical practice will have to change. Quality assurance through adherence to accreditation standards is part of the success formula and a basic requirement for every health care system. However, excellence can only be attained on a patient-by-patient level. All consumers must believe that they are receiving personalized care that is totally focused on meeting or exceeding their defined needs.

The attitude one takes to address excellence in patient care and treatment is often just as important as the technical skill used to treat specific health conditions.[1] Without clear and distinct leadership and proactive participation by physicians at each level within the universe of health care as it's defined today, there will be less effective health care, product-related services, and less than excellence in both the clinical and service quality of the care provided.

Notes

Chapter 2

1. Greenberg, S.B. *Legitimate decision-making at Medica: A survey of Medica members.* Sponsored by the Allina Foundation, Minneapolis, MN, October 6, 1997.

Chapter 4

1. Nelson, A. *Consumer satisfaction evaluation study of ramsey clinic services.* Internal study conducted by Nelson Research Services, Inc., Minneapolis/St. Paul, MN, 1987.

2. Blue Cross and Blue Shield of Minnesota. *How to select a doctor: Tips for health care consumers.* Blue Cross and Blue Shield of Minnesota, Eagan, MN, October 1993.

3. Sommers, P.A. *Consumer satisfaction in medical practice.* The Haworth Press, Binghamton, NY, 1999.

4. Kilmann, R.H. *Management of corporate culture.* John Wiley and Sons, New York, 1988.

5. Silversin, J. and Kornacki, M.J. Employee values and commitment to service. *Medical Group Management Association,* (3) Sept./Oct., 1989.

6. Sommers, P.A. *Medical group management in turbulent times: How physician leadership can optimize health plan, hospital, and medical group performance.* The Haworth Press, Binghamton, New York, 1998.

Chapter 6

1. Hoxie, L. *Department of Ambulatory Healthcare—Accreditation services study.* Joint Commission on Accreditation of Healthcare Organizations, Chicago, January/February 1991; Joint Commission on Accreditation of Healthcare Organizations. *Accreditation Manual for Hospitals* (AMH). JCAHO, Chicago, August 1993.

2. Sommers, P.A. Getting the most out of your visit to the doctor. *Executive Health Report,* 26(1): 1, 4-5, 1989.

Chapter 7

1. Sommers, P. *Medical group management in turbulent times: How physician leadership can optimize health plan, hospital, and medical group performance.* The Haworth Press, Binghamton, NY, 1998.

2. Sommers, P.A. and Luxenberg M.J. Physician-hospital integration Ramsey style. *Minnesota Medicine,* 77: 22-25, 1994.

3. Sommers, P.A. Longitudinal analysis of a physician-hospital collaboration that works: The Ramsey model (1987-1991). *American Medical Group Association,* 43(3): 14, 16-18, 20, 22-23, 26, 55, 1994.

4. Kelly, F.J., Beggs, D.L., and McNeil, K. *Multiple regression approach.* Southern Illinois University Press, Carbondale, IL, 1969.

5. Popham, W.J. *Educational statistics.* Harper and Row, New York, 1967.

6. Sommers, P.A. An inferential evaluation model. *Journal of Educational Technology,* May, 65-67, 1973.

7. Gross, J.C., Joiner, L.M., Holt, L.E., and Sommers, P.A. A kinesio-perceptual test's reliability and validity with retarded subjects. *The Journal of Special Education,* 6(2): 223-231, 1970.

8. Sommers, P.A., Joiner, L.M., Holt, L.E., and Gross, J.C. Reaction time, agility, equilibrium and kinesio-perceptual matching as predictors of intelligence. *Journal of Perceptual and Motor Skills,* 31: 460-462, 1970.

9. Sommers, P.A., Holt, L.E., Joiner, L.M., Gross, J.C., Willis, M.A., and Mainord, J.C. Kinesio-perceptual abilities as predictors of race: A study of the disadvantaged. *The Negro Educational Review,* 21(4): 114-123, 1970.

10. Sommers, P.A. and Fuchs, C. Pediatric care for exceptional children: An inferential procedure utilizing consumer satisfaction information. *Medical Care,* 18(6): 657-667, 1980.

11. Sommers, P.A. Multivariate analysis applied to the delivery of medical services: A focus on evaluation and replication. *International Review of Applied Psychology,* 34(2): 203-224, 1985.

Chapter 8

1. Sommers, P.A and Fuchs, C. Pediatric care for exceptional children: An inferential procedure utilizing consumer satisfaction information. *Medical Care,* 18(6): 657-667, 1980.

2. Sommers, P.A. Active consumer participation in the health delivery system: An evaluation of patient satisfaction. *Bulletin of the Pan American Health Organization* [in English] 16(4): 367-383, 1982; Spanish version in *Boletin de la Oficina Sanitaria Panamericana,* 94(1), Emero, 1983.

3. Sommers, P.A. Multivariate analysis applied to the delivery of medical services: A focus on evaluation and replication, *International Journal of Applied Psychology,* 34: 203-224, 1985.

4. Sommers, P.A. Integrating medicine, education and psychology for children with learning disabilities: The Gundersen Clinic model. *World Pediatrics and Child Care,* 1: 83-95, 1986.

5. Sommers, P.A and Luxenberg, M.G. Physician-hospital integration Ramsey Clinic style. *Minnesota Medicine,* 77: 22-25, April 1994.

6. Sommers, P.A. Longitudinal analyses of a physician-hospital collaboration that works: The RAMSEY model, 1987-1991. *American Medical Group Association:* 43(3): 14, 16-18, 20, 22-23, 26, 55, 1994.

7. Sommers, P.A. Managing medical service outcomes by predicting and achieving success: An inferential approach. *American Medical Group Association*, 42(3): 24, 26-28, 30, May/June 1995.

8. Sommers, P.A., Holt, L.E., Joiner, L.M., Gross J.C., Willis, M., and Mainord, J. Kinesio-perceptual abilities as predictors of race: A study of the disadvantaged. *Negro Educational Review*, June, 114-123, 1970.

9. Sommers, P.A., Holt, L.E., Joiner, L.M., and Gross, J.C. Reaction time, agility, equilibrium, and kinesio-perceptual matching as predictors of intelligence. *Journal of Perceptual and Motor Skills*, June 31: 460-462, 1970.

10. Gross, J.C., Joiner, L.M., Holt, L.E., and Sommers, P.A. A kinesio-perceptual test's reliability and validity with retarded subjects. *Journal of Special Education*, 4(2), 1970.

Chapter 9

1. Sommers, P.A. *Medical group management in turbulent times: How physician leadership can optimize health plan, hospital, and medical group performance.* The Haworth Press, Binghamton, New York, 1998.

2. Stamps, P. Measuring patient satisfaction. *Medical Group Management Association*, 31(1): 36-44, 1984.

3. Kurtz, D. and Boone, L. *Marketing.* The Dryden Press/Holt, Rhinehart Winston, Chicago, 180-185, 1981.

Chapter 11

1. Sommers, P.A. Consumer satisfaction with medical care. *American Medical Group Association,* 29(7): 5-8, 1980.

2. Sommers, P.A. Active consumer participation in the health delivery system: An evaluation of patient satisfaction; *Bulletin of the Pan American Health Care Organization* (English Version), 16(4): 367-383, 1982.

3. Sommers, P.A. Multivariate analysis applied to the delivery of medical services. *International Journal of Applied Psychology*, 34(2): 203-224, 1985.

4. Sommers, P.A. Get the most out of your visit to the doctor. A booklet published by the National Research Bureau, Inc., Employee Communications Division, Burlington, IA, June 1982.

5. Sommers, P.A. *Medical group management in turbulent times: How physician leadership can optimize health plan, hospital, and medical group performance.* The Haworth Press, Binghamton, New York, 1998.

6. Sommers, P.A and Nycz, G. Monitoring consumer satisfaction with clinical services provided to exceptional children. *American Journal of Public Health,* 68(9): 903-905, 1978.

7. Sommers, P.A and Fuchs, C. Pediatric care for exceptional children: An inferential procedure utilizing consumer satisfaction information. *Journal of Medical Care*, 18(6): 657-667, 1980.

8. Sommers, P.A. Managing multispecialty medical services: A focus on special children and the elderly. *Medical Group Management Association*, 31(2): 50-55, 62, 1984.

9. Polit, D.F. and Hungler, B.P. *Nursing research: Principles and methods.* Lippincott Company, Philadelphia, 51-52, 1978.

10. Sommers, P.A. and Theye, F.W. *Dial harmony: A community service of the Comprehensive Child Care Center of the Marshfield Clinic and Medical Foundation, Dial Access Systems: A way to spread your message.* University of Wisconsin Press, Madison, WI, 1979.

11. Sommers, P.A. Evaluation of consumer satisfaction of Gilles de la Tourette syndrome group counseling. Internal study, Marshfield Clinic, Marshfield, WI, 1979.

12. Popham, W.J. *Educational statistics: Use and interpretation.* Harper and Row Publishers, New York, 1967.

13. Draper, N.R. and Smith, H. *Applied regression analysis.* John Wiley and Sons, New York, 1966.

14. Sommers, P.A. An inferential evaluation model. *Journal of Educational Technology*, May, 65-67, 1973.

Chapter 13

1. Sommers, P.A. *Medical group management in turbulent times: How physician leadership can optimize health plan, hospital, and medical group performance.* The Haworth Press, Binghamton, New York, 1998.

2. Joint Commission on Accreditation of Healthcare Organizations (JCAHO). *Accreditation Manual for Hospitals.* One Renaissance Blvd., Oakbrook Terrace, IL 60181, 1997.

3. Kongstvedt, P.R. *The managed health care handbook*, Third edition. Aspen Publishers, Gaithersburg, MD, 1996.

4. National Committee for Quality Assurance (NCQA). *NCQA accreditation process.* 2000 L Street NW, Suite 500, Washington, DC 20036, 1997.

5. Dacso, S.T. and Dacso, C.C. *Managed care answer book,* Second edition. Aspen Publishers, New York, 1997.

6. Sommers, P.A. Getting the most out of your visit to the doctor. *Executive Health Report,* 26(1): 1, 4-5, 1989.

Bibliography

Blue Cross and Blue Shield of Minnesota. *How to select a doctor: Tips for health care consumers.* Blue Cross and Blue Shield of Minnesota, Eagan, MN, October 1993.

Buyers Health Care Action Group (BHCAG). *Request for proposal.* BHCAG, Bloomington, MN, 1997.

Covey, S.R. *The seven habits of highly effective people.* Simon and Schuster, New York, 1989.

Dacso, S.T. and Dacso, C.C. *Managed care answer book.*, Second edition. Aspen Publishers, New York, 1997.

Draper, N.R. and Smith, H. *Applied regression analysis.* John Wiley and Sons, New York, 1966.

Greenberg, S.B. *Legitimate decision-making at Medica: A survey of Medica members.* Sponsored by the Allina Foundation, Minneapolis MN, October 6, 1997.

Gross, J.C., Joiner, L.M., Holt, L.E., and Sommers, P.A. A kinesio-perceptual test's reliability and validity with retarded subjects. *The Journal of Special Education*, 6(2): 223-231, 1970.

Hoxie, L. *Department of Ambulatory Healthcare—Accreditation services study.* Joint Commission on Accreditation of Healthcare Organizations, Chicago, January/February 1991.

Joint Commission on Accreditation of Healthcare Organizations (JCAHO). JCAHO *Accreditation Manual for Hospitals.* One Renaissance Blvd, Oakbrook Terrace, Illinois 60181, 1997.

Kelly, F.J., Beggs, D.L., and McNeil, K. *Multiple regression approach.* Southern Illinois University Press, Carbondale, IL, 1969.

Kilmann, R.H. *Management of corporate culture.* John Wiley and Sons, New York, 1998.

Kongstvedt, P.R. *The managed health care handbook*, Third edition. Aspen Publications Publishers, Gaithersburg, MD, 1996.

Kurtz, D. and Boone, L. *Marketing.* The Dryden Press/Holt, Rhinehart Winston, Chicago, IL, 180-185, 1981.

Mahar, M. *Time for a checkup.* BARRON'S, New York, March 4, 1996, pp. 29-34.

Minser, F. *Guide to creating a clinic environment that exceeds patients' expectations.* Unpublished report written for Consumer Satisfaction Implementation Pilot Project of Allina Health System, Minneapolis, MN, 1998.

National Committee for Quality Assurance (NCQA). *NCQA accreditation process.* 2000 L Street NW, Suite 500, Washington, DC 20036, 1997.

National Committee for Quality Assurance (NCQA). *Accreditation 1999.* NCQA, Washington, DC, 1998-1999.

Nelson, A. *Consumer satisfaction evaluation study of Ramsey Clinic services.* Internal study conducted by Nelson Research Services, Inc., Minneapolis/ St. Paul, MN, 1987.

Polit, D.F. and Hungler, B.P. *Nursing research: Principles and methods.* Lippincott Company, Philadelphia, 51-52, 1978.

Popham, W.J. *Educational statistics: Use and interpretation.* Harper and Row Publishers, New York, 1967.

Silversin, J. and Kornacki, M.J. Employee values and commitment to service. *Medical Group Management Association,* (3) Sept/Oct, 1989.

Sommers, P.A. An inferential evaluation model. *Journal of Educational Technology,* May, 65-67, 1973.

Sommers, P.A. Evaluation of consumer satisfaction of Gilles de la Tourette syndrome group counseling. Internal study, Marshfield Clinic, Marshfield, WI, 1979.

Sommers, P.A. Consumer satisfaction with medical care. *American Medical Group Association,* 29(7): 5-8, 1980.

Sommers, P.A. Active consumer participation in the health delivery system: An evaluation of patient satisfaction. *Bulletin of the Pan American Health Care Organization* (English Version), 16(4): 367-383, 1982.

Sommers, P.A. Get the most out of your visit to the doctor. A booklet published by the National Research Bureau, Inc. Employee Communications Division, Burlington, IA, June 1982.

Sommers, P.A. Managing multi-specialty medical services: A focus on special children and the elderly. *Medical Group Management Association,* 31(2): 50-55, 62, 1984.

Sommers, P.A. Multivariate analysis applied to the delivery of medical services: A focus on evaluation and replication. *International Review of Applied Psychology,* 34(2): 203-224, 1985.

Sommers, P.A. Integrating medicine, education and psychology for children with learning disabilities: The Gundersen Clinic model, *World Pediatrics and Child Care,* 1: 83-95, 1986.

Sommers, P.A. Internal Ramsey study of consumer satisfaction—Nelson Research Service, Burnsville, MN, March 1987.

Sommers, P.A. Getting the most out of your visit to the doctor, *Executive Health Report,* 26 (1): 1, 4-5, 1989.

Sommers, P.A. Malpractice risk and patient relations. *Grand Rounds on Medical Malpractice.* American Medical Association/Harvard Medical Institutions, Inc., Article 1.1, 20-22, 1990 (Originally published in *Journal of Family Practice,* 1985).

Sommers, P.A. Longitudinal analysis of a physician-hospital collaboration that works: The Ramsey model (1987-1991). *American Medical Group Association,* 43(3): 14, 16-18, 20, 22-23, 26, 55, 1994.

Sommers, P.A. Managing medical services outcomes by predicting and achieving success: An inferential approach, *American Medical Group Association,* 42(3): 24, 26-28, 30, May/June, 1995.

Sommers, P.A. *Medical group management in turbulent times: How physician leadership can optimize health plan, hospital, and medical group performance.* The Haworth Press, Binghamton, New York, 1998.

Sommers, P.A. *Alignment: A provider's guide to managing the practice of health care.* The Haworth Press, Inc., Binghamton, NY, 1999.

Sommers, P.A. and Black, K. *Medical group pilot project: Consumer satisfaction redefined in outpatient surgery, pediatrics and internal medicine.* An internal study conducted at Ramsey Clinic and St. Paul Ramsey Medical Center in 1993-1994, St. Paul, MN, 1994.

Sommers, P.A. and Deml, L. *Implementing consumer satisfaction improvement while developing trust with providers for Medica Health Plan members.* 1998 Minnesota Health Services Research Conference, Minneapolis, MN, February 24, 1998.

Sommers, P.A. and Fuchs, C. Pediatric care for exceptional children: An inferential procedure utilizing consumer satisfaction information. *Journal of Medical Care,* 18 (6): 657-667, 1980.

Sommers, P.A., Holt, L.E., Joiner, L.M., Gross, J.C., Willis, M.A., and Mainord, J.C. Kinesio-perceptual abilities as predictors of race: A study of the disadvantaged. *The Negro Educational Review,* June, 114-123, 1970.

Sommers, P.A., Joiner, L.M., Holt, L.E., and Gross, J.C. Reaction time, agility, equilibrium and kinesio-perceptual matching as predictors of intelligence. *Journal of Perceptual and Motor Skills,* 31: 460-462, 1970.

Sommers, P.A. and Luxenberg, M.J. Physician-hospital integration Ramsey clinic style. *Minnesota Medicine,* 77: 22-25, 1994.

Sommers, P.A. and Nycz, G. Monitoring consumer satisfaction with clinical services provided to exceptional children. *American Journal of Public Health,* 68(9): 903-905, 1978.

Sommers, P.A. and Theye, F.W. *Dial harmony: A community service of the Comprehensive Child Care Center of the Marshfield Clinic and Medical Foundation, Dial Access Systems: A way to spread your message.* University of Wisconsin Press, Madison, WI, 1979.

Stamps, P. Measuring patient satisfaction. *Medical Group Management Association,* 31(1): 36-44, 1984.

Watson, G. Interstaff relationships and consumer satisfaction. Unpublished work provided by Results Unlimited, Inc. of St. Paul, MN for *Internal study of implementing consumer satisfaction improvement while developing trust with providers for Medica Health Plan members* (pilot project). Allina Health Systems, Minneapolis, MN, 1998.

Index

Page numbers followed by the letter "f" indicate figures; those followed by the letter "t" indicate tables.

Order Your Own Copy of
This Important Book for Your Personal Library!

CONSUMER SATISFACTION IN MEDICAL PRACTICE

_____in hardbound at $49.95 (ISBN: 0-7890-0713-4)

COST OF BOOKS_____	☐ **BILL ME LATER:** ($5 service charge will be added)
	(Bill-me option is good on US/Canada/Mexico orders only; not good to jobbers, wholesalers, or subscription agencies.)
OUTSIDE USA/CANADA/ MEXICO: ADD 20%_____	
	☐ Check here if billing address is different from shipping address and attach purchase order and billing address information.
POSTAGE & HANDLING_____ (US: $3.00 for first book & $1.25 for each additional book) Outside US: $4.75 for first book & $1.75 for each additional book)	
	Signature_____
SUBTOTAL_____	☐ **PAYMENT ENCLOSED: $**_____
IN CANADA: ADD 7% GST_____	☐ **PLEASE CHARGE TO MY CREDIT CARD.**
STATE TAX_____ (NY, OH & MN residents, please add appropriate local sales tax)	☐ Visa ☐ MasterCard ☐ AmEx ☐ Discover ☐ Diners Club Account #_____
FINAL TOTAL_____ (If paying in Canadian funds, convert using the current exchange rate. UNESCO coupons welcome.)	Exp. Date_____ Signature_____

Prices in US dollars and subject to change without notice.

NAME _____

INSTITUTION _____

ADDRESS _____

CITY _____

STATE/ZIP _____

COUNTRY _____ COUNTY (NY residents only) _____

TEL _____ FAX _____

E-MAIL_____

May we use your e-mail address for confirmations and other types of information? ☐ Yes   ☐ No

Order From Your Local Bookstore or Directly From
The Haworth Press, Inc.
10 Alice Street, Binghamton, New York 13904-1580 • USA
TELEPHONE: 1-800-HAWORTH (1-800-429-6784) / Outside US/Canada: (607) 722-5857
FAX: 1-800-895-0582 / Outside US/Canada: (607) 772-6362
E-mail: getinfo@haworthpressinc.com
PLEASE PHOTOCOPY THIS FORM FOR YOUR PERSONAL USE.

BOF96